NEW TESTAMENT ETHICS

NEW TESTAMENT ETHICS

AN INTRODUCTION

BY

C. A. ANDERSON SCOTT

D.D. CANTAB., HON.D.D. ABER.

formerly Naden Divinity Student
St John's College, Cambridge
Hulsean Prizeman

THE HULSEAN LECTURES

1929

CAMBRIDGE

AT THE UNIVERSITY PRESS

1934

CAMBRIDGE
UNIVERSITY PRESS

University Printing House, Cambridge CB2 8BS, United Kingdom

Cambridge University Press is part of the University of Cambridge.

It furthers the University's mission by disseminating knowledge in the pursuit of education, learning and research at the highest international levels of excellence.

www.cambridge.org
Information on this title: www.cambridge.org/9781107450981

© Cambridge University Press 1934

This publication is in copyright. Subject to statutory exception and to the provisions of relevant collective licensing agreements, no reproduction of any part may take place without the written permission of Cambridge University Press.

First edition 1930
Second edition 1934
First published 1934
First paperback edition 2014

A catalogue record for this publication is available from the British Library

ISBN 978-1-107-45098-1 Paperback

Cambridge University Press has no responsibility for the persistence or accuracy of URLs for external or third-party internet websites referred to in this publication, and does not guarantee that any content on such websites is, or will remain, accurate or appropriate.

Contents

Preface

THE HULSEAN LECTURESHIP, which has been held by many distinguished Churchmen, has hitherto been confined to clergymen of the Church of England. Under a recent statute of the University it has now been thrown open without any such limitation. But this is only the latest stage in a movement which had already led to the opening of the higher degree in Divinity to all, irrespective of their denomination, who are held by competent scholars to be worthy of the Doctorate. These significant steps were taken on the initiative of the Divinity Professors. But they met with the hearty concurrence of the University, as being only consistent with the spirit by which it is characterised, a habit of ignoring all distinctions ecclesiastical and other, and estimating men by the contribution they can severally make to the common life and thought.

As the honour has fallen to me of being the first to enjoy the extended privilege in each case, I welcome the opportunity of recording these changes and acknowledging the spirit by which they have been inspired. The earliest manifestation of that spirit in our ecclesiastical field was seen possibly in the cordiality with which the University authorities welcomed my predecessors when Westminster College was removed to Cambridge in 1899. That cordiality has been continued to their successors. And as it has extended also to our colleagues at Cheshunt College and Wesley House, the Theological Colleges which followed later, it is their express desire to associate themselves with the acknowledgment I now make.

We have specially appreciated the opportunities which have been given to us by the Divinity Faculty of serving as members of the Faculty Board and of the Degree Committee, and as Examiners for the Tripos, and so taking our share in maintaining the tradition of sacred learning in the University.

The lectures which follow appear practically as they were delivered, with the addition of a few paragraphs which were omitted for lack of time.

C. A. S.

WESTMINSTER COLLEGE
February 1930

The opportunity of reprinting has been used for the correction of some mistaken references and for the addition of some Detached Notes and an Index of Texts. I owe the Index to the spontaneous kindness of Donald Matheson, whose memory is still cherished by those who knew him both at Oxford and at Cambridge.

C. A. S.

January 1934

Lecture I

THE MASTER: CHARACTER OF
HIS ETHICAL TEACHING

"FAITHFUL is the saying, and worthy of all acceptation, that Christ Jesus came into the world to save sinners." To save them from what? and to what? The answer commonly given by those who have gone before was, to save them from hell or from the wrath of God, to save them to heaven or to the peace of God. But the modern man, changing the form but not the substance of the thought, answers, to save them from wickedness, to save them into goodness. At the same time it is becoming increasingly clear that this question of goodness *versus* wickedness is one of supreme importance for society. For even God Himself cannot make a good world, a world "fit for heroes to live in", except by making men and women good. And, thirdly, the Christian Church is the only institution in the land which makes it an essential part of its programme to do this great service to the State as well as to the individual, to make men and women good. It is in view of these considerations that I propose to use this opportunity to examine the New Testament teaching on Ethics, the art of a good life, wherein it consists and how it may be attained. It will not be possible in the time available to offer a complete treatment of the subject, collecting and systematising the details. What I shall attempt, and what seems to me of primary importance, is to ascertain and estimate the main principles which underlie the ethical teaching of the New Testament, referring to such details as may be useful for illustration.

We begin with the Synoptic Gospels and the recorded teaching of Jesus of Nazareth. Among the many things which can be predicated of Him not the least important is that He was a teacher. He believed in teaching. It was a form of activity which is recorded of Him more frequently than any other. Unfortunately the records of His teaching which we have in these Gospels are woefully fragmentary and insufficient. But He not only taught far more than has been recorded for us; like all great teachers He taught far more than He put into words. And in estimating His influence we have to think not only of what He directly taught, but of what men indirectly learnt of Him, some of which must have left its mark on their thinking in after days.

It is hardly possible to exaggerate the stupendous difficulty of the task which was undertaken by our Lord—as a teacher; undertaken and partially achieved in a handful of persons while He was yet on earth, achieved more perfectly and on a larger scale after His Death and Resurrection. If we must for convenience draw a distinction between His 'religious' and His 'ethical' teaching (never forgetting how they interlock), we say that in religion He revealed the Father and in ethics the ideal life of man. And by revealed we mean not merely announced or proclaimed, not even demonstrated, but caused men to see, and so to see that they grasped what they saw as great treasure. These things, God as Father and the ideal life of man, became for ever after part of that whereof they were aware. Thus the two *foci* in the ellipse described by His teaching were the Fatherhood of God and the Kingdom of Heaven, by which we may understand the world of spiritual realities and values realised in a social complex. The direction of His influence in this connection and its culmination are indicated by St Paul's discovery that the Kingdom of God is "righteousness and peace and joy in the Holy Ghost".

But Jesus employed also what was practically a synonym for the Kingdom of Heaven as experienced by an individual, when He used with special significance the word "Life". The stages in the Biblical history of this word mark the great stages in the history of religion. Of these the most significant is found in the pregnant sentence in Deuteronomy, "Man doth not live by bread alone, but by every word that proceedeth out of the mouth of

God". Whatever the words were intended to convey in their original context, as used by Jesus in
the Temptation, they mean that man has or has
open to him a life other than that which he shares
with the animal world, a life which is not nourished
by bread. This life, life that is "life indeed"
(1 Tim. vi. 19), life which is unaffected by death, is
nourished by "every word", i.e. by the total self-
communication of God. And again another of our
Lord's intimate friends registered the discovery,
drew the inference from His teaching, "This is life
eternal, that they might know thee...and Jesus
Christ, whom thou hast sent". And he further reports Jesus as eager to give this Life, as calling
Himself the Bread which nourishes this Life; and
the same disciple reports His followers as saying to
Him, "Thou hast the words of eternal life". All
which means that they found that life in the significant sense which He gave to it was first quickened
and then nourished by the total self-communica-
tion of Jesus.

Along these two lines, teaching about the Kingdom of Heaven and teaching about Life, distinct
yet mutually complementary, we discover the revelation given by our Lord as to man and his true
environment and as to the reactions to that environment which were to be looked for when once
its true character was discovered. It was nothing
less than the revelation, the bringing home to man's

consciousness, of the spiritual world, its reality and its incommensurable value. What we call the ethical teaching of Jesus may be seen to consist of practical deductions from the revelation and discovery of man's spiritual environment.[1]

We have been in the habit of speaking of these things as propositions announced and authenticated by Jesus, and then we begin to ask for proofs that they are true and to look for proof in His miracles or in His fulfilment of prophecy. Whereas we ought to begin by recognising a revolution in human thought, accomplished in the minds not of wise and learned men but of fishermen and tax-collectors and harlots. They became aware of God as Father and of the spiritual world as real. And when we ask how was this revolution accomplished, the only answer is, By the authority of Jesus.

What was the nature of that authority? In discussing this question there is one preliminary consideration which still requires to be emphasised, and that is the distinction between coercive and persuasive authority. In popular thought and popular speech the word connotes almost exclusively coercive authority, the authority of force threatened or of force applied. It is indeed the

[1] Compare C. H. Dodd, *Authority of the Bible*, p. 281: "The new thing Jesus gave to men was bound up with what he was. It is not to be formulated in propositions about God, but discerned in the whole new outlook, the new attitude, the new essential relation to God and the Universe which he possessed".

only kind of authority in which the world believes. It is the kind of authority which the world berates the Church for not exercising, claiming or possessing. And it is the kind of authority which Jesus, whether He possessed it or not, definitely and deliberately refrained from employing. He was entirely devoid of the adjuncts which usually accompany such authority—social standing, wealth, organised physical force. His critics put their finger on the absence of such authority as a fatal flaw in his cause. "By what authority doest thou these things?" They gave Him time and again a chance to display authority of this kind in a manner cognate to the claim which they felt Him to be making —"Show us a sign from heaven", from the sky. And He deliberately and repeatedly refused. It was "an evil and an adulterous generation" which demanded a sign, some miraculous portent which would make it, as they thought, impossible for them not to believe. In His Temptation He had rejected in succession three different forms of such coercive authority, and His whole Ministry was consistent with the course to which He then committed Himself. For He knew that not by any kind of coercive authority could faith be created. "Neither will they believe though one rise from the dead."

The stupendous task undertaken and progressively achieved by our Lord as Teacher—the opening of the Kingdom of Heaven, the world of spiritual realities and values, to all believers—was carried out by the exercise of an authority which was persuasive, in part something which proceeded from His character and personality, in part something which appealed to reason or to conscience or to affection. He taught with authority, "and not as the scribes". Not that the scribes taught without authority. Nothing of its kind could exceed the authority claimed by, and conceded to, the scribes. They were the appointed organs of an accepted institution. What the people felt in Jesus was an authority of a different kind. It was an internal authority internally felt. Thus to describe the authority exercised by Jesus as persuasive not coercive is not to suggest that it was hesitating, feeble or ineffective. It carried with it the impression of tremendous urgency, of the vast importance of the issue between acceptance and refusal. It involved a paradoxical synthesis of holy passion and calm. Both, as Frick has pointed out, were rooted in our Lord's consciousness of God. "Herein lies the power of his proclamation of the Kingdom that he takes this God with absolute seriousness, in his holy wrath as well as in his forgiving grace."[1]

The authority which radiated from Jesus was not coercive but persuasive. We must not however

[1] R. Frick, *Der Reich-Gottes Begriff*, p. 7.

forget that there was for the second and subsequent generations a third kind of authority which may be described as experimental. It is the authority which is exercised by an individual or a group which has reacted to a certain teaching or a theory of life in such a way as to put it to the test of experiment, and is thenceforward in a position to confirm it by experience. This is of course the kind of authority by which nine-tenths of our conduct is governed. In innumerable directions it provides us with a working hypothesis, which we accept, in the first instance at least, without question or analysis, and proceed to test for ourselves by experiment. In the field which we are to examine this experimental authority begins to appear in the Apostolic Church, and accumulates as the centuries go on. It is represented on the one hand by the Christian conscience, on the other by the *communis sensus* of the Christian community.

In the region of Christian Ethics its weight and volume become clearly and increasingly perceptible after Pentecost. But it is not entirely unrepresented in the Synoptic Gospels. It has been a mistake on the part of criticism to regard these Gospels as composed in the service of doctrinal propositions or dogmatic tendencies. What is appealed to as evidence of such tendencies is of much more spontaneous origin. The material of these Gospels was collected and moulded by men who had reacted responsively to Jesus. They had to some extent accepted His authority and teaching. These were to some extent confirmed for them by experience. They had, to use the old phrase, "tasted that the Lord is gracious". And many factors or features in the Synoptic Gospels, to which we can assign less historical authority in the strict sense of the word, are of the highest value as reflecting the experimental authority of those who knew Him in the days of His flesh.

But, further, this persuasive authority which radiated from Jesus may be analysed, as it seems to me, into strands or rays which differ from one another in character. It was not uniform in the kind of appeal that it made and makes. Perhaps we shall best realise this if we think of the situation to-day. We come into the circle of Christ's disciples, His pupils, with a general impression that He is one Who speaks with authority on matters of the greatest moment. We have before us the alternative, as most people understand it, either to accept His teaching or to reject it *en bloc*. He is thought of as a Divine Legislator, Whose word can neither be questioned nor criticised, Whose 'commandments' must all be taken literally and must have equal and similar authority with those who accept Him as their Master.

But in practice both questioning and criticism arise in the minds of a large and an increasing number. Are not some of our Lord's demands impossible of fulfilment? Who can produce love to order? Are not others patently inadvisable— "Give to him that asketh of thee"? In the result many compromise, tacitly agreeing with themselves to ignore the awkward imperatives. Many others reject such an impossible scheme of life, and fling themselves out of discipleship. And yet even outside the circle there is in many quarters a wistful sense that after all Jesus knew and taught the secret sources of peace and power, if only we could understand Him.

How if we make the fundamental and fatal mistake in regarding Him as a legislator at all? It was perhaps inevitable that He should come to be so regarded. We see the process beginning and carried pretty far already in the Gospel of Matthew. We see it complete by the time of Cyprian. The treatment of the Gospel as a new law to be literally followed and obeyed by all who claim to be 'saints' was formally adopted by the Anabaptists as one of their principles. There were two strong human motives behind it, the one a natural craving for coercive authority, something 'solid' as men say, something which relieves men of the necessity of striving after spiritual insight; the other due to the reverence with which men look up to Christ as Lord and God, making them chary of claiming the privilege of an ethical insight of

their own. There is a sense in which Christ becomes
for those who commit themselves to Him in faith
an absolute authority

> Whose lightest whisper moves them more
> Than all the rangèd reasons of the world.

But on examination this proves to be the authority
not of His recorded words but of His spirit. It
leaves even such devout followers at liberty to
analyse the character of the authority which they
feel behind His ethical teaching.

A great deal of that teaching is of course conveyed by imperatives, and it is only natural that
men have fallen into the habit of describing these
as our Lord's Commandments, from which it is an
easy step to think of them indiscriminately as all
alike resting on the bare fiat of His authority.
Nevertheless, there is good reason for discrimin-
ating among them, and when we do so, they fall
into three classes. There is first of all the commandment proper, issued on His bare authority,
and of that type of imperative I find only one. It
is of course, "Thou shalt love", "Thou shalt love
the Lord thy God", "Thou shalt love thy neighbour as thyself". Strictly speaking, this was not
original with Jesus. Both the clauses were already
familiar to the Jews in the Law of Moses, the first
in Deuteronomy, the second in Leviticus. And it
is not certain that even their combination was

original with Jesus. It appears three times in the *Testaments of the Twelve Patriarchs*.[1]

But where Jesus shows His originality is that He gave to this twin-imperative a position in His ethical teaching which was absolutely central and creative. It was the same as with the revelation of the Fatherhood of God in the religious sphere of His teaching. That also was not strictly speaking original. But under the influence of Jesus it became a living principle of human thought, conditioning for ever after the conception of God. The twin-imperative takes the same dominating position in our Lord's ethical teaching. According to Matthew's report He followed the enunciation of this principle with the words, "On these two commandments hangs all the law, and the prophets" and it is not too much to say that on them also hangs nearly all that He teaches about character and conduct. The imperative "Thou shalt love" thus occupies a unique position, giving their sanction to all the others, universal in its scope, allowing neither qualification nor abatement, and resting, in the position which our Lord gives it, on His personal authority alone. It makes no appeal to reason. Only those who have accepted can discover support for it in reason. It makes no appeal to conscience, the conscience of

[1] *Issachar* v. 2; vii. 5. *Dan* v. 3. See Abrahams, *Pharisaism and the Gospels*, I. 18 ff.

the natural man. Only the conscience of those who
take it for their standard confirms it as a law of
God. It is rightly described as a commandment,
though I am persuaded that it is the only one of
our Lord's imperatives which can be rightly so
described. It represents the constitution of the
Kingdom. That our Lord had authority to legislate
need not be doubted. But it was not His method.
He did not do it. It was not necessary. For as
St Paul saw and said, "Love is the fulfilling of the
law" (Ro. xiii. 10).

To the significance of this law I shall return at
the close of this lecture. Let us now consider the
other imperatives of Jesus. With a few possible ex-
ceptions they belong to one or other of two types.
Under the first type we have illustrations of how
the single law works, illustrations of its application
to life. Of the imperatives of this type we find a
number gathered together in the Sermon on the
Mount—"Give to him that asketh of thee", and
the rest of the familiar sayings. Sayings of this
type differ from the one Commandment in two
respects. In the first place, we have to make it
clear to ourselves and to others that there is no
obligation upon Christians to understand them or
act upon them literally. To say this is of course to
run counter to a deep-seated and intense conviction
that loyalty to the Master demands our taking Him
at His word. It matters not that there are many

utterances of His which everyone recognises to be figurative. The sense that selfish motives would only be too well gratified to find release of that kind from the pressure of His ethical imperatives honourably restrains His professed followers from having recourse to any explanation that explains away; while at the same time any such explanation provokes sarcastic comment from the unbelieving world. Nevertheless, it cannot be too strongly insisted on that we have express warning from our Lord Himself against this very thing, against always taking Him literally. He never spoke more sharply or more sadly to His Apostles than on one occasion when they had made this mistake. It was immediately after the feeding of the four thousand. They set out together to cross the lake. Jesus began to charge His disciples and to warn them to keep away from "the leaven of the Pharisees" and "the leaven of Herod". They, because of a foolish self-consciousness due to the fact that they had forgotten to take bread, said, "It is because we have forgotten to take bread". And He took them sharply to task. "Do ye not perceive, do ye not comprehend?", because they insisted on taking Him literally. And more than that, He traced their failure to understand, according to Mark's wording, to hardness of heart, spiritual obtuseness; according to Matthew, to insufficiency of faith. If they had been more truly and completely committed to Him, if they had been more sensitive to the working of His mind, they could never have made such a mistake. "How do ye not understand that I spake not to you concerning loaves?" Yet it was in a sense a natural mistake. It is exactly the kind of mistake into which the literalist falls. And the episode should be laid to heart not merely as a justification for our finding figurative language even in our Lord's imperatives, but as a warning that we may wrong Him and only show our own imperfection by doing anything else. We have therefore not only the right but the duty to keep open the possibility that in any particular utterance He may be using a metaphor, a figure of speech, desiring nothing less than to be understood literally.

And so with the hyperboles which He employs. A simple illustration is found in His answer to Peter when he pointed out that he and others had left all to follow Him (Mk. x. 29). Both Matthew and Luke appear to have recognised the hyperbole, and felt the difficulty it creates for the literalist. For while otherwise following Mark very closely they both omit after the words "shall receive a hundredfold" the words "houses, and brethren, and sisters, and mothers, and children". And this is to be "in this present time". No one surely can fail to recognise that what we have here is hyperbole, or to put it frankly, deliberate exaggeration. But for reasons which I have already suggested we shrink from putting a similar interpretation upon Lk. xiv. 26 ff,—"If any man cometh unto me, and hateth not his own father, and mother, and wife, and children...he cannot be my disciple". To take these words literally is to involve our Lord in hopeless self-contradiction, seeing that twice over He cites with emphasis the fifth great commandment, "Honour thy father and thy mother" (Mk. vii. 10; x. 19). If I may venture on a personal reminiscence, any difficulty I might have had about the meaning of this condition of discipleship disappeared in August 1914, when the Sixth Division of the Expeditionary Force mustered on Coldham Common, Cambridge. They were men of between twenty-five and thirty-five, who for the most part had left a wife or a wife and children exposed to all the uncertainties and the hardships of life without them, and to the probability that ere long they would be widows and fatherless. They were acting as if they 'hated' them. Some of them had been told so in so many words. And yet when they shyly pulled out the photographs of wife and children, and showed them to a Cambridge friend, one knew that they had probably never loved them so well as when they obeyed the call of a higher loyalty. We may well let these men interpret for us this saying of our Lord.[1]

---

[1] Compare Dodd, *l.c.* p. 238: "If Jesus said a thing, or even if he were understood to have said it, all experience shows that it is worth while to wait with great humility and patience until the truth in it or behind it declares itself and separates itself from any temporary or relative element".

When we are thus free from the supposed necessity of interpreting literally imperatives of this type, we may learn to see their function as illuminating the application of the single law of love to different situations in life, and doing it by stating the utmost conceivable length to which in given circumstances the application might be carried.

Reserving for our third lecture the detailed consideration of this second type, let us now look at the third. Here we find a number of imperatives (we may take "Seek ye first the kingdom of heaven" as an illustration), where the sanction of the precept is not just the personal authority of Jesus, neither is it a deduction from the universal law. It is of the nature of urgent advice, based largely on the speaker's knowledge of the situation or insight into the case. This distinction between *mandata* and *consilia* was made quite early in the history of Christian Ethics. "Seek ye first the kingdom of heaven" belongs to the class of *consilia*. Jesus took every possible means to press it home, exhibiting with abundant wealth of illustration the character of the Kingdom, its priceless value, the conditions of receiving it or of entering it. In other words, the element of persuasion entered into the authority which He exercised on this subject. And the persuasiveness sprang from His clear vision of immaterial realities, His firm grasp of their incommensurable value. We seek the Kingdom of God not merely because the Master bids us but because He enables us to see it to be the highest goal.

To the same class of *consilia* belong such imperatives as "Sell all that thou hast, and give to the poor". This is a clear instance of prescribing a drastic remedy for an individual case, a *consilium* based on penetrating insight into the moral situation, coupled with a profound recognition of the danger of riches as a bar to sincere seeking of the Kingdom. That does not mean that the case is a rare one. The 'riches' may take many forms besides such as are marketable. And the imperative covers every kind of material possession wherein men come to 'trust', which accordingly becomes a substitute for God. Here the appeal lies not to bare authority, nor yet to reason, but to conscience. The patient recognises the accuracy of the diagnosis. To one like Francis of Assisi the counsel comes home with the authority of a Divine command. It reveals to him in a flash what is the real obstacle to his salvation.

That opens up the question as to the character of the conditions of discipleship which our Lord lays down so emphatically. Are they to be taken literally, and as excluding from discipleship all who do not act upon them literally? There is no difficulty about the first of these conditions. "If any man will come after me, let him deny himself." It ought to be unnecessary to say that what we commonly mean by 'self-denial' or sometimes speak of as 'little self-denials' have little or nothing to do with what Jesus is saying here. He refers of course to the initial and fundamental change, the complete denial of self, by the assertion of God. It is the negative form of the positive command to love. It calls for the continuous and permanent subordination of self-interest to love to God and love to man. The second clause is very difficult, difficult to account for, difficult to explain in its operation. The commentators give very little help. It may be quite true that the spectacle of a criminal on the way to execution carrying his cross was one only too familiar in those days. But that does not account for the use of the word in a metaphorical sense. And no one, I take it, has ever suggested that the words should be taken literally. The Church has surely been right all along in interpreting this condition to mean, let him be prepared to face martyrdom as the possible issue of discipleship, and meanwhile let him accept with cheerfulness all the disabilities, hardships, pains, which the life of discipleship involves. And we have, as it seems to me, a clear indication that this was the interpretation put upon the saying even by the primitive Church in the words which are added by Luke, καθ' ἡμέραν, "let him take up his cross *daily*". The experience adumbrated by the phrase was not one of death but of continuous life as a disciple of Jesus. One has learnt to be chary of ascribing too much in the writings of Luke to the influence of Paul; but is not this a case of the Evangelist interpreting the Master in the light of the Apostle's description of his own experience as a follower of Christ—"I die daily" (1 Cor. xv. 31; cp. 2 Cor. iv. 10)? In fact, the meaning of this demand of Jesus seems to be exactly seized by Paul when he speaks of himself as "bearing about in the body the dying of Jesus". The passage therefore illustrates further not only the fact that such imperatives are not to be taken literally but that the responsibility is thrown on the disciple of discovering how in the circumstances of his life and particularly in view of his calling this condition is to be fulfilled. I say "in view of his *calling*". Not all men were called to 'follow' Jesus in the sense that they must leave all to follow him. Some received such a call as required them to quit home and occupation; others to be celibates "for the kingdom's sake". Others did not, but that neither exempted them from the duty of bearing the cross nor excluded them from discipleship. Once the fundamental change had been accomplished, the denying of self, the witness of conscience would show to each man what bearing the cross meant for him.

To sum up—our Lord's imperatives are not to be taken as together forming a new code of laws.

He sought to substitute life for law, and the observance of ethical standards as the natural expression of life. As Canon Liddon put it long ago: "Although the moral law is eternal, yet under the Gospel it loses the form of external law and becomes an internal principle of life". Jesus did not abolish the old moral laws, but 'fulfilled' them by revealing higher conceptions of duty which lay behind them. He did not abolish the commandment "Thou shalt not kill"; but it becomes irrelevant in a kingdom where a man is in danger of hell who by putting passionate contempt into the word μωρέ, 'fool', kills the brotherly relationship. The path of human duty had been narrowly hedged in by fences of positive law. It has now become the king's highway. The fences are still there but they have been removed to a considerable distance on either side. Only those will come up against them who go far and wilfully astray. "The redeemed of the Lord walk there", hardly conscious of law. For they have accepted the constitution of the Kingdom. They love—not so perfectly as they should—still they love God and they love their fellow-men.

Now what is the meaning of the unique and universal commandment? It is not necessary to do more than point out the most unfortunate handicap under which we labour who seek to commend Christianity to the world in the fact that here at

the very heart of our message stands a word so
ambiguous, so "soiled with all ignoble use". It is
due partly to the poverty of our English tongue at
this point, to the fact that we have only one word
to cover all that the Greek employed two if not
three words to express. And the distance between
the two extremes becomes clear when we realise
that at the one end we may use the word to describe
an emotional disposition which desires nothing so
much as to give, at the other end one which craves
nothing so much as to possess. We say of God that
He "so loved the world that he gave", and equally
we might say of a man, "He so loved...that he
snatched". The two dispositions, either of which
may be connoted by the word, are not only different, they are contradictory, utterly antagonistic
to one another. But apart from the extreme misuse
to which the word may be put, when it means
simply lust, there are all the feeble and sentimental
and romantic associations of the word which re-
quire to be studiously eliminated before we approach its significance in the Christian vocabulary.
And what have we then left? Something which on
analysis reveals three main elements. The first is
recognition, as applied in the two directions which
our Lord indicates, recognition of God and of our
neighbour (the man who is thrown across our
path), recognition of their there-ness and the demand which it creates on our attention. This leads

to the second factor, which is consideration. Love brings its object, whether God or man, into account as a factor in any calculation, any decision which has to be made about conduct. And the third factor is care. Love, *Agapé*, takes its object so to heart that it produces a real concern, an identification of interests, which includes equally the possibilities of joy and pain. As Ritschl puts it, "Love to our neighbours means the identification of self with God's interest in others".

Recognition, consideration, care—beyond this there is even in *Agapé* a certain emotional element which has the effect of establishing a moral union between the subject and the object. But the danger of isolating and over-emphasising this factor is so great that we should guard ourselves against serious misunderstanding if in many passages of the New Testament we rendered the word *Agapé* by 'care'. "Thou shalt care for the Lord thy God with all thy heart." "Thou shalt care for thy neighbour as thyself." The last words of Baron von Hügel were very significant. "Christianity taught us to care. Caring is the greatest thing. Caring matters most."

Our Lord's command therefore is not that we shall love all and sundry in the same way, in the same sense, in which we love those near and dear to us. It is possible, in His sense of the word, to love even those we do not like. And it is possible to accept the commandment in His sense of the word 'love' as a commandment. There are other meanings of the word which make it a matter of taste, of inclination, of psychical attraction, which lie beyond our control. But *Agapé* lies within the control of the will, and it represents that to which our wills are moved by ὁ λόγος τοῦ Χριστοῦ, the message about Christ. And as it is that which our Lord commands, so it is that which He supremely illustrates, that to which the total manifestation of Himself attracts and persuades those who know Him.

It is relevant to ask how the disciples of Jesus were enabled or helped to effect this reversal of the stream of interest in self. As the norm and spring of the highest moral standard the world has known, the command to love rested on the personal authority of Jesus. And we may say that those who accepted Him as their Master thereby committed themselves to the acceptance of His commandment. But in so far as this was evidently far more than an intellectual admission of its validity, in so far as love did begin to manifest itself in them as a controlling power, it was because those who knew Jesus had before their eyes a palmary example of love to God as the inspiration of life, and of love to men as the clue to all the problems of conduct. "We love, because he first loved us" is the simple and sufficient explanation. "Whom not having

seen we love", says another, whether it be Peter
speaking in the name of those who had not seen
and yet had believed, or some one else speaking
for himself as well as for others. And Paul went so
far as to say, "A ban be on anyone who loves not
the Lord" (1 Cor. xvi. 22).

Of course, between the earthly ministry of Jesus
and the use of these expressions stands the death
on Calvary, the purpose and result of which Paul
finds precisely in this, that it commended the love
of God to men. But it was not just any man who
thus commended the love of God; it was one whom
many of those who read Paul's letter had known.
And they found it easier to accept Paul's inference
because they had learnt to love Jesus and loving
Him to love God.

Lecture II

IN the opening chapters of Matthew the Evangelist has collected a number of traditions connected with the birth and infancy of Jesus which had grown up or at least been gathered together subsequently to the formation of Mark and Q. In one of these we find the sentence, "Thou shalt call his name Jesus: for he shall save his people from their sins". Its impressiveness is only increased by its isolation. Its terms find no echo in the Synoptic Gospels, but the rest of the New Testament is full of evidence of the conviction that the promise it conveyed had been fulfilled. For Paul one of the worst consequences of unbelief in Christ as risen from the dead was, "Ye are yet in your sins", under their power and exposed to their consequences. Some may like to think of Matthew's sentence as a proleptic prediction, the vast significance of which remained undisclosed till after the Resurrection. To others it will appear more probable and not less important as a testimony, given quite early in the history of Christian experience, to the moral influence of Jesus, the direction which it took and the power which it exercised. This was the meaning of His Name because this was the result which flowed from His Person. He saved His people from their sins. We have now to consider what He would class as 'sins', the dispositions and actions from which he saved men, before we come to those dispositions and actions which were native to those who had been saved.

At the same time it must be acknowledged from the outset that Jesus is reported as saying very little about sin under that name. It is indeed rather startling to discover that He uses the word only three times in Mark, five times in Matthew and six times in Luke, or, cancelling out the parallels, only seven times in all, and on only three occasions. Moreover, in every case He uses the word in connection with the forgiveness or rather the remission of sins. But we cannot do without a word to describe acts or dispositions which incur the judgment of God, and the natural word to use is the one commonly used in the Scriptures of the Old and New Testaments. Sin is something, whether act or disposition, which injuriously affects a man's relation to God.

We wish to discover therefore what were the acts and dispositions which according to the teaching of Jesus incur the judgment of God, and the consequences which He predicated. Our sources of information fall into three main types:

(1) such meanings as are found in Mk. ix. 42–48, (2) the passage about what defiles a man [Mk. vii. 14–19], and (3) the denunciations of specific offences largely directed against the Pharisees, and generally associated with the word 'hypocrites'. In these contexts we are to see the forms of conduct and disposition which Jesus regarded as evil, and also to learn something of the consequences which He foresaw as following such conduct.

Some thirty years ago certain divines made the discovery that "Jesus did not denounce sin". It was a discovery which appeared to give them a joyful satisfaction. They proceeded to proclaim it loudly and widely. But though superficially true, it rested on two falsities of method. It involved a misleading insistence on the word 'denounce', as though it were an exhaustive description of reaction against evil. Whereas what Jesus had to say about sin was thrown into forms very different from those adopted by many who have subsequently spoken in His name. In that very limited sense the saying was true. But, secondly, it put an arbitrary limitation on the meaning of 'sin', confining it in effect to what is popularly included in the term. These divines, in effect, brought a ready-made catalogue of what they and the world thought of as 'sin', comprising mainly dishonesty, intemperance and impurity, and comparing it with the recorded teaching of Jesus found no passage in which He, in so many words, 'denounced' these things. Whereas, had they considered the evidence as to our Lord's total reaction to evil they would have discovered that one of the things He does for us is to widen and deepen our conception of it almost to the point of transforming it. For the popular conception of sin, even to this day and even in the light of our Lord's teaching, hardly goes beyond the breach of the sixth, seventh and eighth commandments, as expanded more or less in their application by His teaching.

In strict literalness it is true that He did not 'denounce' those 'sins of the flesh' which in the popular estimation almost exhaust the contents of 'sin'. But it is equally true that even in regard to these He did something much more impressive. He recognised the appalling danger to which men expose themselves by cherishing and cultivating the dispositions and appetites of which these things are the fruit. And He sought to bring that danger home to them even by the use of startling hyperbole. "If thy hand, thy foot, thine eye, causeth thee to stumble." If, that is, in your case these members have become the organs of evil dispositions, evil appetites, "cut them off", "pluck them out"; words which we should wrong our Lord by attempting to take literally. What they are evidently intended to convey is that no constraint can be too drastic to be put on physical members which

thus become the organs of evil. Whether or not
Paul has this teaching of Jesus before his mind, he
gives its correct interpretation: "Present not your
members to sin as instruments of wickedness, but
present...your members to God as instruments
of righteousness" (Ro. vi. 13). For, adds Jesus, it is
better to enter into Life with one hand, one foot
or one eye, than having both to be thrown into
Gehenna. The alternatives are stated in terms which
with ever-deepening meaning had been current in
Jewish thought since the time of Deuteronomy:
"Behold, I have set before you life and death".
And just as Jesus in this passage offers the current
phrase "the kingdom of heaven" as a synonym
for 'Life', so he puts 'Gehenna' for 'death'. The
class of sins which he has here in view and the
dispositions from which they spring have this fatal
consequence, that they shut a man out from Life or
the Kingdom of Heaven. Of that he was sure, and
it would be difficult to find language more solemnly
deterrent of these sins, sins of the flesh as we call
them, than what he uses here. Such sins were an
obstacle, a fatal obstacle, to Life.

In the same context (Mk. ix. 42) we find evil
conduct of a different type handled in the same
way. To cause "one of these little ones" to stumble,
by teaching or example, to make it difficult for
the innocent to keep their innocence, for the weak
to walk upright in the ways of God—for one who

did that it were better that he were plunged in
the depths of the sea. The alternative is here expressed in terms of physical death; but it is such
as to press home the responsibility of every man for
the moral freedom of his brother, especially the
ignorant and the weak, and the value amounting
to sacredness of every man as a moral personality.

Another passage which throws important light
upon our Lord's conception of what we call sin,
what He included in it, and the consequences by
which it is attended is in Mk. vii. 14–23, the section
about defilement. Here the ordinary reader probably does injustice to the Pharisees because he
naturally gives a moral meaning to the word
'defile'. To such it suggests moral delinquency,
conduct that leaves a stain upon the conscience.
But the Pharisees, whatever may have been the
ethical obtuseness of some of them, had more intelligence than to believe that contact with a dead
body, for example, had a defiling effect on a man's
soul. But their method of concentrating attention
on the external and ritual conditions of religious
privilege lifted the weight off such witness as they
bore to the "other things", mercy and justice and
loyalty, the internal and moral conditions of really
spiritual privilege.

What the Pharisees meant, when they said that
such contact with objects which were ritually unclean 'defiled' a man, was that it disqualified him

from public worship, from taking part in the public sacrifices, from the normal means of approach to God; e.g. Num. xix. 16, "Whosoever in the open field toucheth a grave shall be unclean seven days". As Johannes Weiss puts it, he becomes "separated from God, is excluded from the sanctuary and segregated from the sacred community".[1] It has often been said that our Lord never spoke words which were more revolutionary than those in which He definitely and emphatically repudiated this teaching. He laid the axe at the root of legalism. But He did so by emphasising the ultimate or deepest meaning of the word rendered 'defile'. What really disqualifies a man for fellowship with God is never anything that enters into him, never any kind of food that may be ritually 'unclean', but it is the things that come from a man, the manifestations of evil disposition which really have this effect. They disqualify him for fellowship with God.

What then according to our Lord are the things which have this disastrous effect? We are familiar with the list given in Mk. vii. 21, 22. But it deserves careful study. After the comprehensive phrase "evil confabulations" alluding to the half-conscious discussions within a divided mind, "letting 'I dare not' wait upon 'I would'", we find a group which describes more clearly the

[1] Joh. Weiss, *Urchristentum*, p. 136.

sins, the grosser sins as we call them, at such times as we remember that there are others. Breaches of the moral law as laid down by Moses 'defile' a man. But this group is followed by a series which carries us far beyond Moses, carries us into a field in which the evil disposition or temper is at least of as much account as the evil act, and specifies among the things that defile a man not a few towards which the Christian conscience is still apt to be indifferent. Among these are πλεονεξίαι, manifestations of possessiveness or insatiableness. Dr Moffatt translates 'lust', limiting (unduly as it seems to me) the significance of the word to one particular aspect of possessiveness. The word describes an attitude towards material goods of every kind directly opposite to that demanded by Jesus. Then follows malice, deceit and jealousy. And it is only necessary to study an obstinate or advanced case of any of these in order to discover that He was right. These are in fact dispositions which do injuriously affect, and in the end destroy, our relation to God. The three with which the list closes deserve special attention. ὑπερηφανία is frequently rendered 'pride', but it is pride which hurts, the assumption of superiority which involves 'despising others'. St Luke found a natural expression of it in the words of the Pharisee in the parable, "I thank thee that I am not as other men, or even as this publican". The English versions all render βλασφημία by 'blasphemy', a word which in our usage connotes defiant and injurious speech against God and that only. But while it may be doubted whether that is even part of the meaning here, it certainly refers and probably refers only to violent and insulting speech directed against men. It has always been and still is an unhappy characteristic of social life in Eastern lands that men on the slightest provocation break out on one another in violent abuse. We may find an illustration in the word "Fool" in Mt. v. 22. The man who says to his brother "Raca" exposes himself to prosecution for slander before the local court, but the man who says μωρέ exposes himself to the danger of hell. Not of course by the mere pronunciation of the word, but by the temper of which it may be made the vehicle and expression. It breaks fellowship. Vituperation, scurrilous insult directed against a brother-man, that also "defiles". And the list closes with ἀφροσύνη. This is usually translated 'folly', and most of us must have been conscious of a sense of anti-climax or bathos when we read or heard this word at the end of the list. Nevertheless it is a true climax. For we must take the word in the sense which·is abundantly illustrated in the Old Testament. There is connotes not so much intellectual stupidity as moral obtuseness.

We find a crucial example of this significance of

the word in the story of Nabal, whose name meant
Fool, and folly was with him. Both the conduct
and the claim of David may be open to criticism
from the standpoint of civilised ethics. But there
can be no doubt that in the ethical judgment of
the time he had by protecting Nabal's flocks
established a moral claim upon him, a claim for
recompense. And when Nabal scornfully repudiated any such claim, he manifested what in the
Old Testament is called 'folly', the contemptuous
refusal to recognise a moral obligation. And we
should do well to translate ἀφροσύνη here as
'moral insensibility'. That also defiles a man, disqualifies him for fellowship unto God. And so, far
from finding an anti-climax here, we recognise a
true climax, if it be not also a suggestive summary
of what has gone before, corresponding to a
similar summary at the end of Eph. iv, "and grieve
not the holy Spirit of God"—in any of these ways.
In fact, we have here an instructive parallel to
what our Lord says elsewhere about the sin against
the Holy Spirit which has no forgiveness. For
moral insensibility, which grows upon the man who
consistently rejects the claims of goodness or of
grace, becomes something for which there is no
remedy. It is not that God refuses to forgive, or
even fails to offer forgiveness, but that forgiveness
has become something which cannot reach him.
He is impervious to it through moral insensibility.

Consideration of this list of actions and dispositions prompting actions which our Lord would have men classify as sins, suggests some important inferences. In the first place there are only three or four of these twelve forms of evil against which it would be possible to quote a written law. The others, so far as Jesus may be said to be looking to the past as well as to the future, could be criticised only on the ground of the common moral sense of a religious community. In the second chapter of Amos we hear the prophet pronouncing doom on the king of Moab because he had "burned the bones of the king of Edom into lime". There was no written law to forbid such conduct, but it was already repudiated by an unwritten law of humanity. And by the voice of His prophet God endorsed the repudiation. So Jesus by His own authority endorses the judgment of the religious conscience that these actions and dispositions are evil.

In the second place, if we are right in throwing the emphasis in $\beta\lambda\alpha\sigma\phi\eta\mu\iota\alpha$ upon vituperation of other men, every one of the actions and dispositions here proclaimed to have the effect of sin represents injury done by a man to his fellow-man. So far is it from being true, as is assiduously maintained in some quarters, that it is the honour and dignity of God which is primarily challenged by sin. Ask a fourth-form boy what he understands by sin, and he may well reply, "Sin is doing what we would

like to do, but mustn't". "Why mustn't you?"
"Because it is forbidden." "Who has forbidden
it?" "God." "Why has God forbidden it?"
"God only knows." The moral obligations of the
Christian are not infrequently represented as "a
bundle of prohibitions", enunciated for mysterious
reasons by a jealous and arbitrary Deity. Yet this
passage stands here to show (and this is true of
the New Testament teaching on the subject as a
whole) that such an account of sin is wholly mistaken. What we see here is that God takes under
His protection the well-being and true happiness
of men whether as individuals or in the group, e.g.
the family. Wrong done to these is wrong done to
God. In other words, what we call nowadays anti-
social action falls under the category of sin. It
involves more than the victim who suffers by it.
It recoils upon the evil-doer. It disqualifies him
for fellowship with God, or, as we shall see later,
according to St Paul it disqualifies him for the
Kingdom of God. "They that do such things
cannot inherit the kingdom".

Even actions that still seem to us trivial in comparison with what we recognise as sin are neither
unimportant nor isolated. They represent the self-
expression of that universal kingdom of evil which
God has set Himself to overcome. They belong to
the works of darkness which Jesus came to destroy.
And that our Lord proclaims this so emphatically

is not due to any arbitrary judgment or to any desire to pursue human conduct into meticulous details. It is due to his clear vision of reality, the values that belong to human life and must be protected if it is to be truly happy.[1] What Browning predicates of Lazarus, the man who had been in heaven, may illustrate the ethical standpoint of one who was always in heaven: "Heaven opened to a soul while yet on earth, Earth forced on man's use while seeing heaven....Should his child sicken unto death—why look for scarce abatement of his cheerfulness, while a word, a gesture from that same child at play, or laid asleep, or in the school, will startle him to an agony of fear".

The third direction in which we may look for light upon our Lord's judgment on conduct is in the specific causes which roused indignation in Him and in the specific charges which He brought against the Pharisees. Mark tells us of three occasions when He was moved to anger or indignation. "He looked round about on them with anger, being grieved at the hardening of their heart" (Mk. iii. 5). He had just put to the men in the synagogue the question, "Is it lawful on the Sabbath day to do good or to do evil, to save life or to kill?" And by their silence they revealed an obstinate deter-

---

[1] God embodies in His character the very values after which men long, including the dignity and freedom of personality. Gal. v. 21; cf. 1 Cor. vi. 9; Eph. v. 5.

mination not to see or to admit that they saw the truth of the answer which He expected. Obstinate prejudice rendered them blind to truth. As He reminded them on another occasion, there was not one of them who would not even on the Sabbath day drag his ox or his ass out of a pit into which it had fallen; but they would not admit that it was lawful to heal a human being (Lk. xiv. 5). On two other occasions Mark tells us that Jesus manifested indignation, one when the disciples tried to hinder the women from bringing their little ones to Him, and another when His anger blazed forth at the exploiting of the Temple and its worship for priestly gain. Thus we see His anger kindled by inhumanity claiming the sanction of religion; by the misrepresentation of religion involved in making it an excuse for such inhumanity; by the privileged blocking access to their privileges for those whom they looked on as inferior; by religion turned into a means of oppression of the many and aggrandisement for the few.

On these occasions we find our Lord's indignation falling upon the people, the disciples and the Temple-rulers. And the moral blunders which he scourged in the Pharisees were not essentially different in kind; blocking the way to God (they had taken away the key of the Kingdom of Heaven); devouring widows' houses (using legal rights of foreclosure without any considerations of humanity); despising others ("this people that knoweth not the Law is accursed"), pretending to dissociate themselves from their fathers who killed the prophets while they treated them and their message as dead. "These are the things with which God is angry every day, and it is a sin in men if they can look on them without indignation. To keep people ignorant of religious truth, neither living by it ourselves nor letting them do so; to raise recruits for our own faction on the pretence of enlisting men for the Kingdom of God; to destroy the sense of proportion in morals by making morality a matter of law in which all things stand on the same level, these are the things which caused a storm of anger to sweep over the soul of Jesus."[1]

Was our Lord justified in thus associating such conduct specially with the Pharisees? Is the picture of them which we get from the Synoptic Gospels true to the facts of the first century? It is obviously not possible to go fully into these difficult questions. But they must be at least touched on, seeing that the denial that the picture is a true one or that His denunciations were justified is widely heard from authoritative scholars, and tends, so far as it is accepted, to discredit the historicity of the Gospels, and ultimately to discredit our Lord's authority. Christian scholars have given an attentive and respectful hearing to

[1] Denney in *Dict. of Christ and the Gospels*, I. 61.

those representatives of Jewish scholarship like Dr Claude Montefiore who have done their utmost to show that the representation of the Pharisees in the Gospels is unfair, prejudiced and untrue to the facts. And this has been done, especially by Dr Montefiore, with such learning, such a sincere effort after impartiality and such genuine respect for Jesus as he conceives Him to have been, that counter-criticism has been almost disarmed. But the veracity and ultimately the honour of our Lord are at stake, and we cannot allow judgment to go by default. One thing we ought frankly to recognise and admit, namely, that we have been mistaken, the Christian Church as a whole, in looking on all the Pharisees of our Lord's time as falling under His condemnation, culpably mistaken in identifying 'Pharisee' with 'hypocrite', in assuming that there were not good Pharisees as well as bad, though we might have to say that they were good in spite of their system rather than because of it.

But when that is admitted it must be frankly said first that the only strictly contemporary evidence on the subject is that furnished by the Synoptic Gospels, and further that the catastrophe of A.D. 70 with the final destruction of the Temple and the cessation of priesthood and sacrifices was followed by such changes in Judaism, and by the emergence into influence of so many new ideas and ideals, that it is more than ever precarious to read back evidence from the close of the century or later into the situation in the first three decades.

And secondly, the very favourable picture of Pharisaism which is drawn by some Jewish scholars is by no means accepted by all of them. It is indeed a subject of almost bitter controversy among their leading scholars to-day. Authorities like Moritz Friedländer take an entirely opposite view of the Pharisees in the time of our Lord, and find nothing which we read of them in the Gospels too dark for the facts. Thus, "Not only Sadduceeism but Pharisaism had become wholly worldly and waded deep in the crassest materialism and hypocrisy". Or again, "The canker of the century bore the name of Pharisaism". The question, Who are meant by the Minim? is a very difficult one, and one on which those who are not well-read in Rabbinic literature can only keep silence, but it is a tenable theory that they were at least a group within the Pharisaic sect, and if so the Talmud itself contains attacks on them as violent as anything in the Gospels. "Jesus himself", says Friedländer, "did not say anything worse of these destroyers of the world."[1] In the absence of really contemporary evidence outside the Gospels, and in view of the contradictory opinions put forth by

[1] M. Friedländer, *Die rel. Bewegungen innerhalb des Judentums*, pp. 89, 110, 112.

Jewish authorities themselves, it would certainly appear that there is no sufficient reason here to doubt the existence in Gospel times of a considerable body of Pharisees whose life and conduct gave only too good ground for our Lord's criticism.

And the severity of that criticism is both explained and justified by the position which they occupied. It was not only that they discredited the religion of which they were the recognised representatives, by their sham piety, the hypocrisy which allowed such a glaring contrast between their professions and their practice. What made the situation far more serious was that they represented a system directly inimical to the conceptions and teaching of Jesus, one from which men must be delivered before they could enter the Kingdom[1]; and here the hypocritical Pharisees would be joined by the others who were not hypocrites in our sense of the word. The type of character which they represented was the natural product of a mistaken idea of God and of the way to deserve and obtain His favour. Its governing principle lay in the idea that by keeping the Law in all its details and even going beyond its requirements, by fasting twice in the week when once was all that was required, by paying tithes not only on the crops but on the trumpery kitchen herbs, men could establish a claim upon God. It

[1] As Paul died to the Law, Ro. vii. 4, 6.

was a fatal perversion of religion to teach that men could earn the favour and forgiveness of God. It crystallised and helped to propagate a false conception of God. It obscured, if it did not deny, the prophetic revelation of God, as "merciful and gracious, long-suffering and abundant in goodness and truth", as One Who "desired mercy and not sacrifice". In a word, it stood squarely in the way of the revelation which Jesus was striving to communicate to men, and it was associated in many individual members of the party with a type of character which all men are agreed in regarding as contemptible. The force of our Lord's denunciations of the Pharisaism which embodied these false conceptions and produced this type of character is fully explained by that passion for righteousness which He shared with the old prophets and His passion for the men who were in danger of being robbed of their inheritance in the Kingdom by the Pharisaic system.

I have already suggested that there is a distinction, and I think it is an important one, between the meaning which we give to the word 'hypocrite' and the meaning in which, on some occasions at least, Jesus employed the word. In several of the passages in which persons are addressed as 'hypocrites' what they are charged with is difficult to associate with deceit, even with self-deceit or conscious inconsistency. Take for example Lk. xii. 56,

"Ye hypocrites, ye know how to discern the face of the earth and the sky, but ye discern not this time of opportunity". Dr Moffatt twice renders the word by 'irreligious' and twice by 'impious'. I cannot see in either rendering more than an unsuccessful attempt to recognise that our word 'hypocrite' is not entirely satisfactory. For hypocrisy as our Lord saw it included something much subtler than the pretence of bad men to be good. It was subtler even than the self-deceit of those who thought they were good while many of their actions were really evil. To confine hypocrisy within these limits would be to make it consist of moral obliquity alone. And as illustrated by our Lord's own teaching it is seen to contain an intellectual element as well. It was not only a failure on the part of men who made a great profession of religion to do what they knew to be good, it was a failure to think out the practical application of their religious principles in their relations with other men. In other words, we cannot evade the application of the description to ourselves by the comfortable assurance, which with good reason we cherish, that we are not hypocrites in the common significance of the word. Let me give some illustrations. In the common sense of the word no one of the men I am going to mention was a hypocrite, and yet one asks whether in certain particulars they would not be so classified by Jesus; Richard

Baxter, when he said, "A man must be a very obdurate Sadducee who would not believe in witchcraft"; John Wesley, when he said, "Giving up witchcraft is in effect giving up the Bible"; Martin Luther, when he said, "He that says slavery is opposed to Christianity is a liar"; the Moravians in Germany (than whom no Christian community has earned a nobler reputation for their piety, self-sacrifice and zeal for the Kingdom), when they wrote to the Moravians in America, "If you take slaves in faith with the intention to conduct them to Christ, it shall not be a sin but may prove a blessing"; George Whitefield, when he persuaded the trustees of Georgia to introduce slavery—"I should think myself highly favoured if I could purchase a good number of slaves, in order to make their lives comfortable [and lay a foundation for bringing up their posterity in the nurture and admonition of the Lord]".

One does not cite these cases in order to cast a slur on these great and good men, least of all to plume ourselves on any moral superiority over them, but solely in order to press home the point that 'hypocrisy' in the full sense our Lord gave to the word is far commoner than we have imagined. One asks indeed whether any of us is free from it, and one dimly foresees a time when the Church of a future age will be as amazed as we are when we look back, because of the propositions to which we too readily commit ourselves, such as, "You can never get rid of war", "It is the people who make the slums", "Prostitution is a necessary evil".

We should do well to define a 'hypocrite' in our Lord's sense of the word as one who refuses the guidance of the Holy Spirit in the application of the principle of love to duty—remembering that the refusal is generally due to love of something else than God.

Lecture III

THE MASTER: HIS METHOD
OF GOODNESS

W^E turn now to some general aspects of our Lord's ethical teaching. One or two of these are so familiar that it is not necessary to do much more than mention them. The first is the steady pressure with which He pushes back behind the evil action to the evil disposition of which it is the fruit, a disposition which He sees to involve even worse consequences than the actions which spring from it. Thus He contrasts murder with angry passion, adultery with gloating lust. It is not merely that the disposition comes into the reckoning as well as the act, but that it is judged and entails its consequences prior to, and it may be independently of, any overt action at all. And a distinction becomes possible between a single act of sin, due to sudden temptation or inexperience when a man, to use Paul's phrase, is "overtaken in a fault" and acts of sin which, whether single or habitual, are the genuine expression of an evil disposition. As Weinel says, "The instant the moral requirement rises to such a height that it becomes a demand for a good disposition, it is clear that ethics have reached a great turning point in their development".[1]

A second characteristic of our Lord's ethical teaching which is commonly recognised is His way of pushing back behind the current form of Mosaic law to the initial principle of which that law was the expression. It is thus that He deals with the law of the Sabbath, claiming in effect that its application is to be governed by the purpose for which it was instituted; "The Sabbath was made for man". And it is thus that he deals with the question of divorce, reaching back behind the Mosaic sanction of divorce by the husband even on trivial grounds to the essential character of marriage as revealed in the original constitution of man and woman. This of course ante-dates any legal or ceremonial recognition of marriage. What it means is that there is in the sexual relationship itself a union of personalities which no man will break who orders his life according to the will of God. With reference to what is known as the exception (παρεκτὸς λόγου πορνείας), I may say that I agree with the judgment given by a great Anglican authority that no critical investigation will ever decide whether the Lucan text which omits the words or the Matthean text which inserts them is the authentic report of what Jesus said. On the other hand, I agree with those who hold that whether He used the words

[1] Weinel, *Jesus or Christ*, p. 37.

or not they are probably true to His meaning. When the marriage bond has been inwardly repudiated by πορνεία, our Lord's followers are not prohibited from giving formal effect to the breach by divorce.

When we come to consider the ethical teaching of Jesus on its positive side, we are struck by the comparative absence of independent detail as regards the ethical qualities and experiences to be looked for in His followers. When I say 'comparative' I mean in comparison with what we find in Paul, as well as in other teachers of ethics. And when I say 'independent' I mean what does not derive directly from the single law of love. In Paul we have, for example, a rich variety of motives, standards and qualities of conduct predicated of the Christian. In Jesus we have the big all-inclusive ideas, "Thou shalt love", "So shall ye be children of your father", with a number of illustrations of the conduct implied in the command and leading to the glorious privilege.

In the Beatitudes, Matthew has collected together a number of very significant sayings, by a combination of which we get an invaluable though by no means complete outline of our Lord's ideal for human character. He pronounces 'blessed' those who manifest certain aspects of character, eight in all. Once more He is proclaiming what He sees to be true, rather than saying what becomes

true because He says it. Indeed, we might do well
to bring this out, by translating μακάριοι in each
case not by "Blessed are" but by "Ah, the happiness" of the poor in spirit and so on, just as we
should do well to render οὐαί in the so-called
"Woes upon the Pharisees", which again sounds
like a *fiat*, by "Ah! the misery". The Beatitudes
themselves fall into two groups, one of four belonging to the religious, the other of four belonging
to the ethical, sphere. Jesus recognises as the truly
and eternally happy those who acknowledge their
spiritual poverty, those to whom the evil that is in
the world is a continual grief and pain, who in
fact have taken up the cross, those who yearn after
goodness, and those who make no claim (οἱ πραεῖς),
but cast themselves upon the mercy of God. It
belongs to the essential character of the Kingdom
that they who thus commit themselves to God shall
find the conditions they have accepted here reversed there. In the same manner, He pronounces
happy those who are compassionate (like the
Good Samaritan and unlike the Unmerciful Servant), those who are "pure in heart", a phrase
which we must not limit to what we call moral
purity, but expand to include freedom from
worldliness and self-interest, those who make around
them an atmosphere of peace and that not merely
as the opposite of strife but in the wider sense of
outward and inward tranquillity and tranquil-

lising power,[1] and those (if the eighth beatitude belongs to the original series) who patiently endure persecution for the Gospel's sake. What Jesus predicts concerning those who manifest these qualities is not, as in the former sayings, the reversal of the previous condition but its natural issue. The merciful have their hearts open to mercy. The pure in heart have the pure vision of God. Those who radiate peace are recognised as belonging to the family of God. Those who participate in the sufferings of the Kingdom share also in its triumph.

These and other similar utterances of Jesus raise the question of reward. It is easy on a superficial reading of such passages to conclude that He encourages moral effort by the offer of rewards, that in fact He is back at the old Jewish point of view of obedience establishing a claim for Divine recognition. But, in the first place, it is very doubtful whether the absence of what it is only natural to describe as reward is after all a mark of the highest ethical system. It would rather appear that in a universe directed to moral ends good action and good character must issue in satisfaction. And, secondly, if even in the highest ethical system there must be such satisfactions, the real questions are, what is the nature of these satisfactions, and in what degree are they set forth as inducements? And while, in answer to the second question, it

[1] See Joh. Weiss in *Schriften des Neuen Testaments, ad loc.*

cannot be said that Jesus does more than reveal
what He sees to be the issues of ethical development and self-sacrifice, the satisfactions which He
foretells are such as would appeal to those only
who had reached a high level of ethical and religious development. As it is well put by Frick
in a recent work: "The Kingdom of God is an
inheritance which the Father prepares for His
children, a reward which the Lord gives to His
servants. Jesus rejects the ethic of desert, but He
never rejected the idea that loyalty in service is
worthy of and receives reward. The deed must
never be looking to the reward, but the reward
surpasses the deed a hundred-fold. And wherein
does the reward consist? Properly speaking, in
the Kingdom of heaven itself".[1] And neither that
Kingdom nor any of the detailed satisfactions into
which it can be analysed, for example, "righteousness and peace and joy in the Holy Ghost", as
Paul puts it, make any appeal except to the man
who has given primary value to the Kingdom in
his thinking and his life. In other words, the
'rewards' attached to Christian conduct and character are not discontinuous with these but being of
like quality have the appearance of springing out of
them, though they are really the gift of God who

[1] Cp. Frick, *Geschichte des Reich-Gottes-Gedankens*, p. 16. On
the same question in connection with St Paul's teaching see von
Soden in *Zeitschrift für Theologie und Kirche*, 1892, p. 117.

"is not unfaithful to forget your work and labour of love". "Precisely those parables which speak of reward make it specially clear that all reward is after all only grace. The parable of the Labourers in the Vineyard 'slays the reward-idea while it applies it' (Holtzmann)."[1]

I have said that most of our Lord's imperatives, so far as they are addressed to all His followers alike, are best understood as applications of the law of love to specific situations in life. But many of them are at the same time prompted by the desire to save His followers from what He saw to be great moral dangers. And among these the two with which He seems to have been most deeply concerned are vindictiveness and possessiveness. These, more than any other evil dispositions, were seen by Him to put a gulf between men and the Kingdom, between men and God. Vindictiveness in the form of refusal to forgive finds its type in the Unmerciful Servant, as possessiveness does in the figure of Dives. It is the dread of vindictiveness as a poison fatal to the moral nature which lies at the back of His teaching about human forgiveness. His standpoint differs here from ours. When there is presented to us a case which calls for forgiveness, our interest focuses on the one who has done the wrong. Fellow-feeling leads us to reason in his favour. He is the victim of environment. He acted

[1] Frick, *ut cit.* p. 8.

on impulse. He did not know what he was doing. We want him to be forgiven. Jesus, on the other hand, appears curiously indifferent to the party who requires forgiveness. All His interest is concentrated on the one who has the opportunity to forgive. What will he make of it? Will he be able to conquer the vindictiveness natural to the natural man? So much hangs upon it; for forgiveness of injuries inflicted by man is a condition of being forgiven by God. The picture is not of God standing on His dignity, as it were, and saying: "If you do not forgive men their trespasses against you, I will not forgive your trespasses against Me". God's forgiveness is for His repentant children; but the filial spirit towards God involves the brotherly spirit towards all who call God Father.[1] To cherish pride and resentment and refuse to acknowledge family claims is tantamount to admitting that we do not belong to the family and are not fit for forgiveness. The point of view to which Jesus would lead His followers is that any wrong done to one of them offers an opportunity for him to forgive; whether the forgiveness becomes effective in the experience of the doer of wrong depends on whether he repents.

It ought not to be necessary to point out that this condemnation of vindictiveness does not carry with it a condemnation of anger. But the modern

[1] J. F. Macfadyen, *Jesus and Life*, p. 182.

humanitarian interpretation of Jesus tends both to ignore the fact that this perfect man could be angry, and also to condemn and discourage anger in His followers, thereby robbing the Church of a God-given instrument for the defence of righteousness. To ignore the fact that Jesus could be angry is to ignore the evidence of the Gospels,[1] and it is to close our minds to a study of the conditions under which anger is not only justified but called for. In itself anger may be either a vice or a virtue. It is according to circumstances. What makes it a vice is, as Aristotle puts it,[2] when men are angry on wrong grounds, or with the wrong people, or in a wrong way, or for too long a time.

When we collect and examine all the relevant passages, we "may infer that the two things in human conduct which moved Jesus most quickly and most deeply to anger were (1) inhumanity, wrong done to the needs and rights of men; and (2) misrepresentation of God by professedly religious people and especially by religious teachers".[3] When His anger kindles, it is always in defence of others; it is absolutely pure from personal feeling, and it does not destroy even temporarily His love for those on whom it falls. Though anger is often

[1] E.g. Mk. iii. 5; x. 13; xi. 15, besides many passages in which we feel the presence of anger, thought it is not described.

[2] *Ethics*, IV. 5, 7.

[3] See James Denney, 'Anger' in *Dictionary of Christ and the Gospels*.

sinful, the absence of anger may be due to the
absence of love; and the man who can see 'the
little ones' made to stumble and who takes it
quite coolly is very far from the Kingdom of God.
It is relevant to recall that the fierceness which
came to animate the Suffragette Movement in 1914
was partly due to the refusal on the part of men to
be angry at the horrors perpetrated on women and
children by those of their own sex. The attitude
required by Christians is summarised by St Paul
in Eph. iv. 26, where he enjoins anger, but adds a
strong warning of the danger of being angry in a
sinful way, and lays a ban upon vindictiveness,
"Let not the sun go down upon your wrath".
Anger, as Thomas Fuller said, is one of the sinews
of the soul.

The portrait of the unforgiving man which is
drawn with such scathing precision in the Unmerciful Servant has its counterpart in the portrait
of Dives. His sin is not that he is rich. There is
no reason to think that Jesus countenanced that
opinion. It is that he trusted in his riches and that
he hardened his heart against the silent appeal o.
the beggar who was laid at his gate. He experienced the "deceitfulness of riches". The security
which he found in the consciousness of material
possessions proved to be illusory. It was swept
away by death. The callous satisfaction which he
felt in the superiority which his riches gave him

over Lazarus was completely reversed under the conditions of the world to come. Jesus led no crusade against property or against those who had it. But he left no doubt as to the fearful danger of their position as He saw it, the insidious power of possessions of any kind to lead a man to trust in something else than God, to degrade him into a mere acquisitive animal and ultimately to make him immune to the appeal of human need. This πλεονεξία or possessiveness, which Paul so penetratingly equated with immorality on the one hand and with idolatry on the other, was one of the characteristics which Jesus branded as disqualifying a man for fellowship with God.

Confining ourselves still to our Lord's direct teaching on ethical subjects, it appears to me that much of it can be usefully grouped under two general maxims, of which the first is, "Do not press for your rights". That does not mean, deny or even forget that you have rights. They are part of your inheritance, part of your value. But do not make them a ground of claim. Let your relation to them be such that you are always prepared to waive them. This was indeed the relation of Jesus Himself to what may be called *His* rights. It is the meaning of the word πραΰς (A.V. 'meek') which He applies to Himself ("I am meek and lowly in heart"), which Paul also registers as one of His marked characteristics ("I beseech you by the

meekness...of Christ"), the absence of self-
assertion which is quite consistent with a deep
sense of personal value and dignity. And we see
the same illustrated in His conduct. When officious
men came to Peter and asked whether his Master
paid the tribute-money, the Temple-tax, and
Peter referred the question to Jesus, His first reply
involved the assertion of a tremendous claim.
"The kings of the earth, from whom do they collect
tribute, from their sons, or from strangers?" And
on Peter's replying, "From strangers", Jesus concludes, "Then the sons are free". His meaning is
clear. He claims such a relationship to God for
Whose worship the tribute is collected, that it is
unreasonable to expect Him to contribute to the
maintenance of that worship. He makes the claim,
but promptly waives it. "Nevertheless, lest we
should shock them...give unto them for me and
thee" (Mt. xvii. 24–27).

We see the working of the same principle on an
important occasion, when our Lord presents Himself for Baptism. It was a repentance-baptism for
the remission of sins, a symbol also of admittance to
the community of the coming Messiah. It postulated
repentance, a complete change of attitude, it offered
ceremonial cleansing, it sealed a new relationship.
But Jesus was free from the necessity of professing
the first or seeking the others. Personal repentance
was both unnecessary and impossible for Him. It

was indeed to His point of view that those who repented at least partially conformed. And in so far as the repentance to which remission of sins was granted involved sorrow over the past, there was no room for that in His consciousness—except vicariously. Further, He needed no initiation to the Messianic kingdom. For was He not its King? Had He claimed His rights, the rights attached to His personality, He would have remained aloof, spectator of others' baptism. But He waived these rights, for "it behoved him to be in all things like unto his brethren". He did it determinedly, and did it, as we know, at great risk, the risk of his action being misunderstood, as it is to this day. He Who "thought it not a thing to be clutched at to be equal with God" insisted that He should not seem to be superior to men. He was already so united to them in sacrificial love that He was willing to be seen as one with them when they professed repentance or change of mind. This 'meekness' of Jesus which showed itself perpetually in the small concerns of daily life, and runs back through striking incidents such as these to the Incarnation itself, is what our Lord commends to men when He in effect bids them claim less than their rights.

That is the first point which throws light upon His teaching on non-resistance as we call it; the second is that men should look on vindictiveness,

resentment, as a fell moral disease; and the third
is that, as He Himself warns us, we have to be
watchful for occasions when He is not to be understood literally.

He begins by reminding men of their rights, Jews
of the rights conferred upon them by the law of
Moses, as they understood it the law of God. It
was their right to exact "an eye for an eye and a
tooth for a tooth". Of course when that law was
first promulgated, it marked a great advance on
the earlier law or practice of the desert. That
authorised retribution or revenge which was practically unlimited This sternly enjoined a limit. Only
an eye for an eye and a tooth for a tooth. Still, it
gave each man the right to gratify the vindictive
spirit. "But I say unto you, resist not evil."

The familiar translation is unfortunate, although
it is fundamentally right in taking the adjective as
neuter not masculine. That is to say it is not, as
some have thought, the evil man or the evil one
who is not to be resisted, but malicious wrong.
But the familiar words are ambiguous, suggesting
far too wide an application and covering a meaning
against which Scripture and conscience alike pro-
test, such as that the followers of Jesus are not to
resist evil of any kind in any way. The primary
reference at any rate is to personal wrong, to
malicious injury inflicted by a personal enemy.
"Withstand not wrong." Do not let it bring you

into the ring. On the contrary, "whosoever striketh thee on the right cheek, turn to him the other also".

The first objection to taking these words literally is that they become so unimportant, seeing that, literally speaking, the case seldom or never happens, at least among civilized people. But of course no one does take these words with exact literalness. Everyone extends them to cover any kind of physical attack. And our Lord's advice is that we should say to the attacker in effect, "Go on". That is, to begin with, apt to be disconcerting to him who attacks. It puts a distinction between him and his victim which makes him uncomfortable. It may be the beginning of new things for him. "The attacker expects your resistance; if you do not resist, your rejection of his challenge may enter the situation with the force of a new idea."[1] That is no doubt true and has its importance, but it would be rash to suppose that it touches the major purpose behind the imperative. Here also our Lord's interest is concentrated on the man who is attacked, that he shall deal with the situation rightly. It is in fact his opportunity, as Schiller saw:

> Der Feind kann mir auch nützen,
> Er sagt mir was ich soll.

> Even my foe can do me service,
> From him I learn my task.

[1] Hocking, *Human Nature and its Re-making*, p. 374.

If he meets the attack with the natural instinct of resentment and returns blow for blow, he allows the evil man not only the satisfaction of the blow but the satisfaction of dragging him down to his level; he drops out of the kinship of God. Thus, in effect, the law recognised by unredeemed humanity, even the law of Moses, gives you the right to retaliate. But do not claim that right. Rather take up such an attitude to your enemy that in the extreme conceivable case it would be natural for you, were it likely to secure your end, to turn the other cheek. And the end or ambition which Jesus sets before His follower in such circumstances is that he may "gain his brother" (Mt. xviii. 15). But it is not necessary to look further than St Paul for the just interpretation of these words. "Why do ye not rather put up with injury? Why do ye not rather allow yourselves to be defrauded?" (1 Cor. vi. 7); "Be not overcome by the evil, but overcome the evil with the good" (Ro. xii. 21). Neither will it be supposed by anyone that this is to suggest a softening or reduction of our Lord's demand. It is to bring within the range of common experience what otherwise would lie outside it, to substitute for a demand for action which is but rarely called for, the demand for a temper or disposition which continually finds opportunities for exercise. And it is a disposition which is native to those who really care for their neighbour.

We may take a second illustration from the same context, "Give to him that asketh of thee", words which in themselves cannot and must not be explained away. They mean, Give to him that asks what he asks and when he asks it. And if they were to be literally applied would be open to all the obvious and well-grounded objections with which we are familiar. They are to be understood literally, but not literally applied. Once more, Jesus is dealing with what is understood to be one of man's natural rights, the right to have property, the right to do what he likes with his own. It is to be observed that Jesus nowhere denies this right. It may be correct to speak of Him as a revolutionary. But if so He is a revolutionary in morals not in economics, however possible it may be that a wide extension of His revolution in morals would lead to an economic revolution too. He did not contemplate the community of those who attached themselves to Him as having stripped itself of all individual possessions. He is even at pains to instruct His followers what they shall do when they "make a feast". Jesus admits the right to hold property. But He bids men waive that right, bids them hold it as not holding it. We have recognised the alarming danger which He saw to attach to the holding of riches, but also that it was not all His followers whom He urged to get rid of them. But to them all He said, "Give to him that asketh of thee".

"Are you to give to everyone that asketh you? Certainly not. But pay your poor rates willingly; don't try to cut down wages to a minimum; and give all the help you can to individuals you know who are out of work because there is no work for them to do." So has Dr Bethune-Baker answered the question,[1] and I would add, let your mind and conscience be sensitive to the silent appeals which come to you from those whom you are in a position to help, not only of the needy and the sick, but, for example, the young man in your employment who is anxious to get on, to climb the ladder behind you. In other words, do not press your claim to have and to hold property, money-power, as your own. Rather take up to it such an attitude that it will never in itself be a hindrance to your giving help to your neighbour, even at cost to yourself. Seek opportunities of what von Hügel was so fond of calling "costing service". This also will be natural if you care for your neighbour.

It is relevant to observe that our Lord Himself did not fulfil this precept with literalness. There can be little doubt that He reserved the right to discriminate among those who came asking Him for help and healing. That at least appears to be the meaning of the saying: "He did not many mighty works there because of their unbelief". In that instance at least He limited His beneficence

[1] Bethune-Baker, *The Way of Modernism*, p. 36.

A S   5

not of course because the people failed to believe
that He was this or that, but because they refused
to commit themselves to Him to the extent that
they could receive from Him something more and
more important than the material boon. The same
consideration must often operate in directing or
limiting Christian giving. "The gift without the
giver is bare", not only for him who thus gives
imperfectly but for him who receives imperfectly
the gift without the giver. And the principle received ecclesiastical sanction in the Lambeth
Report on Spiritual Healing. "It is not the busi-
ness of the Church to apply its means of restoration
if no higher end is sought than the recovery of
physical health."

These illustrations confirm what I have said as
to the necessity of watching lest we misunderstand
our Lord by taking Him literally, also as to His
insistent demand that His followers should be
wholly free from vindictiveness and possessiveness,
and as to the mighty and sufficient motive being
found in 'caring'.

A second general precept which lies behind our
Lord's teaching may be put in a similar form. It
is, "Do more than your duties", with the corollary,
"Do even your duties in a different spirit".
"Except your righteousness (or goodness) surpass
that of the scribes and Pharisees, ye shall not enter
into the kingdom of heaven" must have sounded a

hard saying. For in the estimate of those who heard it the righteousness of the Pharisees was something which few of the poorer and less cultivated class need hope to attain, not to speak of surpassing it. Practical religion being largely conceived of in terms of the performance of external religious duties, of almsgiving and good works, for which a certain amount of leisure and wealth were indispensable, the obligations devised and accepted by the Pharisees must needs appear beyond the reach of many who were disposed to be religious. Yet Jesus calls upon all and sundry as a condition of entering the Kingdom to display goodness even in excess of theirs. Evidently He means goodness of a different, a superior quality. And St Luke records an occasion when Jesus gave teaching which, perplexing as it has been to many, brings out the significance of this demand. It is where He raises the question of how any of His hearers would treat a servant at the end of his day's work. Would he send him at once to get his own meal. Far from it, he would make him work on till he himself was satisfied. "So likewise ye, when ye shall have done all those things which are commanded you, say, We are unprofitable servants: we have done that which was our duty to do" (Lk. xvii. 10)—"a highly noble, notable and important passage" as Dr Montefiore calls it. The key to its meaning lies in the word 'servant' (δοῦλος). For it is of the slave or perchance the hireling, and of those who perform their duties in the slave—or hireling—spirit, that the words are true. It is indeed the mark of a slave that he can never be 'profitable', in the sense of producing a margin beyond what his master has a right to expect of him. Every hour of his time, every ounce of his strength belongs to his master. He can never do more than it is his duty to do. A curiously close parallel is provided for us by Seneca, who asks, "Can a slave confer a benefit? Is his service, however lavish, not merely a duty to his lord, which as it springs from constraint, is undeserving of gratitude?"[1] On the other hand, the position is reversed when even the same work, the same duty, is performed by a son in the spirit of a son. The very first hour of the son's service, the first output of his energy, is 'profitable' to the father. He rejoices in the manifestation of filial loyalty and eagerness to please. It is not fashionable to quote Ruskin nowadays, but his teaching on this matter ought not to be allowed to die. "If your work is first with you and your fee second, work is your master and the lord of work, who is God. But if your fee is first with you and your work second, fee is your master and the lord of fee, who is the devil. And it makes a difference now and ever whether you serve him who has on his vesture written 'King of kings' and whose service is

[1] Seneca, *de Ben.* III. 18.

perfect freedom or him on whose vesture is written 'Slave of slaves' and whose service is perfect slavery."[1] The principle applies equally to duty done by constraint and to duty done for reward. Love prompts and inspires to do more than duty and to do all that is done in the spirit of sonship, "all for love and nothing for reward". The converse is crystallised in the vigorous apophthegm of Edward Thring: "Quench love by saying, pay up your pound and I will give you a receipt for duty done".

The same summons to do more than our duties finds further illustration in the Sermon on the Mount. "Whosoever shall compel thee to go one mile, go with him twain." The situation springs out of some compulsory duty. Some one has been pressed for service, possibly by a tyrannical overseer of public works. He is ordered to go one mile. Do more than what you cannot help doing, says Jesus; "go with him twain". Is there not something distinctly humorous in the situation thus created? The overseer is enjoying his brief authority. Suddenly the positions are reversed. The man does not stop at the end of the first mile. He goes on for a second. Amazement of the overseer. By so doing the man transforms the whole character of his work. He shows that he has done it, even the first mile, not as the unwilling victim

---

[1] Ruskin, *Unto this last*, p. 57.

of the *corvée*, but as a free man conferring a favour. True dignity and true freedom belong to the man who does more than he has contracted to do. He works out of good-will, not of compulsion. In the sphere of morals his righteousness 'surpasses' the righteousness of the Pharisees. He does more than his duties, because he does his duties differently. The Christian does them differently because, as St Paul puts it, he has exchanged the spirit of servitude for the spirit of sonship (Ro. viii. 15).

It is beyond my purpose and obviously beyond the scope of these lectures to give a complete account of our Lord's ethical teaching. I have tried to illustrate His method and to exhibit some of the underlying principles. I am only afraid that I may still have left ground for the impression that in some sublimated way the imperatives of Jesus form at least the equivalent of a code of laws. It is the almost inevitable result of taking them one by one. These imperatives are there, and must be always of the highest value. But perhaps we allow them to serve us best if we allow them to outline for us the character of Jesus Himself, the reaction of His will to different moral problems as they arise. For there can be no manner of doubt that what He taught He practised. His followers not only heard Him describe the characteristics of the ideal; they saw it daily before their eyes. To recapture the impression they received is the final task in the study of the ethics of the Gospels.

There is a saying of Westermarck which appears apposite here. "We must not confuse the moral law with the moral ideal. Duty is the minimum of morality; the supreme moral ideal of the best man is its maximum."[1] May I use an illustration of my own? All games which deserve the name are provided with laws. And the first condition of playing the game is that we know the laws and obey them. But all the best games are provided with something more. That more may be described as the etiquette of the game. And the etiquette is even more important than the laws. The penalties for neglecting it are more serious, much more serious than the penalties for breach of the laws. How then do we learn the etiquette? Is it not by playing with the best people? So life has its laws; but it has also its etiquette. And many things which are not forbidden by the laws are sternly banned by the etiquette. And defiance of etiquette in this sphere also has even more serious consequences than breach of the law. How then are we to learn the etiquette of life? Is it not by living with the best people? Is it not, in the ultimate resort, by companying with Jesus Christ? In other words, the portrait of His character which gradually yields itself up to patient study becomes our moral

[1] *Cit.* Montefiore, *The Old Testament and After*, p. 264.

guide, the ideal not as an object of admiration merely, but as the living force of personality entering into our consciousness and directing our wills. We call it His Spirit. The laws remain, as I have said, but to the man who has this living energising ideal, the Spirit of Christ, in his heart, they are like sign-posts to one who knows the road.

Lecture IV

"WE have the mind of Christ." So said the Apostle, and one of the strangest phenomena in the New Testament is to be observed in the evidence that there was so much to justify the claim. Such evidence is not lacking in the sphere of religious thought, and for the sphere of ethics it is copious. Of course it is possible that when he writes "we" the phrase is to be taken as including others besides himself, but the probability is that he uses the word here as elsewhere of himself alone, that is to say of one who had not even been among the disciples of Jesus. On the other hand, it is possible, even probable, that Paul was not wholly without knowledge of Jesus in the days of His flesh. They appear to have been born within a year or two of one another. And the only traditions which we have concerning Paul's early manhood appear to make him resident in Jerusalem at the time of our Lord's Trial and Crucifixion. For they bring him to Jerusalem while still a youth (Acts xxvi. 4), make

him a pupil in the theological college of which
Gamaliel was the head, and show him, without
a break, occupying a prominent position among
those who were only too zealous for the law at the
martyrdom of Stephen. "If Paul was not acci-
dentally absent from Jerusalem, scarcely anything
else is possible than that he himself saw Jesus there
and was perhaps present at his execution."[1] That
is the conclusion of von Dobschütz, and Feine in
his great study of Paul speaks of him as a witness
of the Crucifixion.[2] To me it appears that that
would go far to explain the tone of the Apostle's
allusion to "the blood" of Christ. It is not the
tone of one who is working with a theologoumenon
(contrast the writer to the Hebrews) but a tone of
mingled awe and horror, as of one who had seen it.

I cannot agree with Loofs, who, while thinking
it probable that Paul had seen Jesus, does not
believe that the question is very important. For,
if he did see Him at the crisis of His fate, the Trial
and Crucifixion, the mingled majesty and gentleness of the Victim would leave an impression which
was not only indelible but pregnant of strange consequences.

---

[1] See von Dobschütz, *Der Apostel Paulus*, p. 50. The same view
is maintained by J. H. Moulton and Ramsay, by Joh. Weiss,
Paul and Jesus, pp. 28 ff., and specially by Feine, *Neutestamentliche
Theologie*, pp. 431 ff. It is regarded as "improbable" by A. S.
Peake, *Bulletin of John Rylands Library*, July 1928, p. 8.

[2] Feine, *Der Apostel Paulus*, p. 434.

But Paul had to rely for his knowledge of what Jesus did and said, of the impression that He made, upon what he learnt from those who had actually been His disciples. And during the fifteen or twenty years between his conversion and the writing of his Epistles he must have had many opportunities of conversing with such. The Synoptic Gospels had not yet taken shape, but the material out of which they were to be composed was passing from man to man, from group to group, and was crystallising into connected narratives. There is no reason in the nature of things why Paul should not be acquainted with most of the contents of these Gospels and *with much else* of what the Lord Jesus had done and taught. Nevertheless it is not in that sense that he had "the mind of Christ", or that he shows that he had it. Very rarely does he quote words of Jesus, or refer to any but what may be called the outstanding experiences of His life. Indeed, a somewhat superficial criticism has drawn the inference that Paul had little knowledge of, and less interest in, the historical Jesus. And yet the fact remains that a portrait of an ideal Christian drawn from material supplied by St Paul would not differ in any important feature from the portrait similarly drawn from the teaching of Jesus. Paul may supplement but he never contradicts his Master. And precisely those features which are most characteristic in the one are those which most distinguish the other. And yet it is not the material provided by Jesus which is reproduced. Much of the Apostle's teaching seems to represent teaching of Jesus which has passed through the alembic of his own mind. Much more can only be described as the work of one who, having taken up the same attitude as Jesus to God and to the world, standing as it were by His side, sees things as He saw them and carries on the application of His principles to new conditions and problems of conduct.

The first illustration of perfect harmony between Paul and his Master is a very obvious one, the importance of which is apt to be obscured by its obviousness. It is the way in which Paul makes *Agapé* or caring the master-key to all problems of social relationship. The same compelling and controlling force which had moved God to give His Son, which had moved Christ to give Himself, could be trusted to move men to all needed subordination and sacrifice of self. For Paul, as for Jesus, the function of *Agapé* in the moral life was both central and all-comprehensive. "All the law is fulfilled in one word, even in this; Thou shalt love thy neighbour as thyself" (Gal. v. 14). "He that loveth his neighbour hath fulfilled the law" (Ro. xiii. 8). "Above all things put on *Agapé*, which gives cohesion to the perfect life" (Col. iii. 14). It is a sufficient criticism of un-ethical or un-Christian conduct to say, "Your behaviour is no longer inspired by love" (Ro. xiv. 15). And, of course, Paul is not alone in this, but is joined by John, especially in his first Epistle, and by "Peter" in his first Epistle. There is a note of triumphant confidence in John's words where he registers the fact that "We love, because he first loved us" (1 John iv. 19); and he actually points to *Agapé* as the criterion of salvation, "We know that we have passed from death unto life, because we love the brethren". But it is Paul who develops the application of this indwelling force to character and conduct. And because of its bearing on the Christian's relations to his fellow-men, he rejoices perpetually to recognise its presence and its activity among those to whom he writes—among the Thessalonians (1. i. 3), the Corinthians (2. viii. 7), the Ephesians (i. 25), the Colossians (i. 4) and in Philemon (5). He urges upon the Romans (xiii. 8), the Galatians (v. 13) and the Philippians (i. 9) that they should "abound in love". For the sacred Society is "rooted and grounded in love". Love is the basis on which it rests, the soil from which it draws its nourishment.

The second illustration is much less obvious, so much so that many will be inclined to deny its validity. It is to be discovered in the fundamentally similar attitude to the Law taken up by Jesus and by Paul. I say 'fundamentally similar', because some of the forms in which Paul's attitude to the Law finds expression suggest divergence rather than harmony. Paul speaks of the preaching of the Cross as the great stumbling-block which hindered Jews from accepting the Gospel. But whatever may have been the case when he was preaching, there can be little doubt that in subsequent history it has been his criticism of the Law which has made him and his teaching specially obnoxious to the Jews. And even Christian scholars lose patience with the Apostle in what Schweitzer calls his "peculiarly inconsistent attitude to the Law". Once more it is not difficult to feel sympathy with Jewish students of Christianity, who think of Paul as one who delivered violent attacks on what is the palladium of their race. For the Law is to the Jew far more than a legislative Code. It is hardly too much to say that it occupies for the Jew the place occupied by Christ for us. It is the undying mediator between God and man. It communicates the mind of God to man, and provides and regulates the approach of man to God. It is not surprising therefore that the attitude of the Jew to the Law has at times approached one of worship, or that he has always regarded Paul's teaching on the subject as insolent heresy.

Yet Paul had an immense respect for the Law. He spoke of it as "holy and just and good". He declared that it was "spiritual", that it belonged

to the spirit-world, almost equivalent to speaking
of it as Divine. He reckoned among the inalienable
privileges of Israel that it had "the legislation".
He said even of circumcision, ὠφελεῖ, "it has its
value". He continued to practise some even of its
ceremonial observances. If therefore we find him
at the same time proclaiming that "Christ is the
end of the Law", rejoicing that he and other
Christians have been made dead to the Law,
proving to his own satisfaction that the Law was
inherently relative and transitory (Gal. iii. 19 f.),
the charge of inconsistency is not unnatural. But it
is not mere inconsistency. It is a paradox deeply
rooted in Paul's discovery of Christ and His
gospel of free salvation. And it rests on the fact
that the Apostle views the Law in two aspects.
He views it in its contents as making known the
ethical requirements of God, and as such it is
"holy and just and good". But he views it also
as a system, the exclusive emphasis on which encourages men to think that by slavishly obeying
it they can command the favour of God and earn
their own righteousness. As such it was the direct
contradiction of the gospel with which Paul had
been entrusted, the embodiment of a system to
which Christ had put an end. And something of
his vehemence is accounted for by his own experience of the Law, the promise of life which it
had held out, and the bitter disillusionment of

the discovery that the promise was vain. Jesus had no such experience.

But the same paradox had been already observable in the attitude of Jesus to the Law, and in His teaching. Luke brings the two extremes into close juxtaposition (Lk. xvi. 16, 17). "It is easier for heaven and earth to pass away, than for one jot or tittle of the law to fail", words which immediately follow the statement of the converse, "The law and the prophets were until John: since that time the kingdom of God is preached", something which transcended the Law. Matthew reports Jesus as saying, "I am not come to destroy the law", even as Paul repudiates the same suggestion, "Do we then make void the law through faith? God forbid: yea, we establish the law" (Ro. iii. 31). But Matthew proceeds at once to show how Jesus criticised the Law, interpreted some of it so as to abrogate it. We hear Him practically leaving the law of the Sabbath to be interpreted by the individual conscience, and in His teaching about defilement undermining a great part of the ritual law, and that not the least important in the eyes of the Pharisees. We hear Him anticipating Paul in proclaiming the relative character of the Mosaic legislation. "Moses for the hardness of your heart suffered you to put away your wives." And the Apostle's reiterated argument about works and faith, about law and grace, which is apt to strike the modern reader as wearisome logomachy, is after all only an elaboration into systematic form of the teaching of Jesus in the parable of the Pharisee and the Publican. The man who went down to his house justified rather than the other, was the one who made no claim on the ground of his 'works' (boasting is excluded—Ro. iii. 27) but cast himself on the mercy or grace of God, exercising simple faith.

If, therefore, St Paul's attitude to the Law seems inconsistent or paradoxical, so does also that of our Lord. And that makes it all the more remarkable that the attitude in both cases was practically the same. With regard to our Lord, it has been well asked, "May not the truth be that in the depth and range of his insight he was more fully aware of continuity with tradition than his most conservative followers, and more aware of the newness of what he taught than the most radical?"[1] In Paul we find the same double attitude drawn out into clear expression; and nowhere more clearly than in the words which run in the A.V. "the letter killeth, but the spirit giveth life" (2 Cor. iii. 6). We both misunderstand and misapply these words when we assign to them a distinction between keeping the law in the letter and keeping it in the spirit. Paul's meaning is far otherwise. We should do well to translate, "The written code killeth

[1] C. H. Dodd, *ut cit.* p. 278.

(any written code); the spirit maketh alive". If the effect of our Lord's teaching was to urge men to substitute life for law, it was Paul's triumphant conviction that they had been delivered from bondage to a written code and committed to the guidance of the living Spirit[1] (cp. Ro. vii. 6).

Had St Paul been asked what was the authority behind the ethical teaching and decisions which he gave he would surely have replied, the authority of the Holy Spirit, or what was in practice synonymous for him, the authority of the Living Christ, "the Christ that speaketh in me" (2 Cor. xiii. 3). But this did not mean, unless in exceptional circumstances, a mere intuition unaided, uninstructed, unrelated to a moral or historical context. He sought and accepted material for his judgment in the Law and the Prophets, in the reported teaching of Jesus and in the character and example of Jesus as it was known to him. On one occasion he is careful to make clear when he passes from what rests on the teaching of Jesus to what has only his authority behind it (1 Cor. vii. 10, 12). But that is a case of what we might call literary conscientiousness, making it clear that what he

---

[1] The distinction was tersely expressed in a work of the seventeenth century which had great influence on the ecclesiastical development of Scotland, *The Marrow of Modern Divinity*: "Both these laws [of Moses and of Christ] agree in saying, Do this. But there is this difference. The one saith, Do this and live. The other says, Live and do this. The one says, Do this for life. The other says, Do this from life".

was now saying could not claim confirmation from the past.

But what is even more important is that Paul believed and taught that those who were truly Christian had the power to discover for themselves what was the will of God, especially in matters of conduct. For it was open to them to be so "renewed in their mind" that they could "ascertain what is the Will of God—the Good, the Well-pleasing and the Ideal" (Ro. xii. 2).[1] Christians are to be guided, as they have been emancipated, by "the spirit-principle that leads to life in Christ Jesus".[2]

We start, therefore, with a remarkable harmony between Paul and Jesus in their fixing on *Agapé* as the all-comprehensive force for good in conduct and in their double attitude to the Law, recognising the validity of its contents, but claiming the right and power to know and ascertain the will of God independently of the Law and sometimes even in contradiction to its formal meaning. Now these matters in which they were at one are fundamental. And they account, especially the first of them, for much of the harmony in detail between Paul's ethical teaching and that of his Master.

---

[1] See Weiss, *Urchristentum*, p. 432: "It is exceedingly important that the renewing of the mind which takes place through the Holy Spirit is to find its expression just in this that the Christians have a clear sense of that which is the will of God".

[2] "the law of the spirit of life in Christ Jesus." Weiss renders νόμος by 'Macht'.

While the correspondences between the thought of Jesus and that of Paul on ethical matters are many and obvious, the differences are few and subtle. Perhaps the most important of these has to do with sin and forgiveness. Their respective handling of forgiveness throws light upon divergent conceptions of sin. In all of His reported references to the subject of forgiveness our Lord speaks of it in terms of "the remission of sins". That is to say, He appears to look at it in a forensic aspect. The sinner is one who has incurred guilt, has been convicted, whose conviction is recorded against him. And forgiveness stands for the cancelling of the conviction, the removal of the guilt. The result is that the sinner returns to the class of the innocent—but not, so far as appears, to a restored personal relation.

When we come to Paul we find the same conception lying at the back of his doctrine of Justification (expressed, however, in a different vocabulary), the δικαιοσύνη θεοῦ, the need of it and the bestowal of it. But we find also what I can only call a deeper conception of sin and a deeper conception of forgiveness. For he introduces a new term for forgiveness, one which occurs only once in the Synoptic Gospels, χαρίζομαι. It is a term which ignores the forensic aspect, and emphasises the personal relation, once destroyed, now restored— "even as God in Christ hath forgiven you" (Eph. iv. 32).

It is here that we find light on Paul's deeper conception of sin. It is something which calls not merely for acquittal, but for reconciliation. Concerning 'sin' itself, under that name, and in the sense we give to that word, he too has very little to say. For him sin is almost always an external force which he all but personifies. It is existent and active prior to its effecting a lodgment in the human soul. It is "death's sting", used by Death (also personified) as the dragon of fable used its sting to pierce the body of a victim and inject its venom. But underlying his conception of forgiveness and reconciliation we find this conception of sin, deeper than what comes to expression in the Gospels. If we want to find evidence of the same conception in the mind of Jesus, it must be in the parable of the Prodigal Son. And if we want to find an explanation of the fact that the Apostle, apparently advancing beyond the Master, gave this meaning to sin and forgiveness, this primary place to reconciliation, we may find it in Paul's effort to explain the significance of the death of Jesus. He saw Him set forth upon the Cross as ἱλαστήριον, that is as one with power to restore friendship[1]; bound up with that was the conviction that the worst result of sin must be seen in the destruction of the true relation between God and man, the highest result of our Lord's sacrifice in its restoration. Sin was not merely breach of law,

[1] See *Christianity according to St Paul*, pp. 67 ff.

it was breach of fellowship—as in the case of the Elder Brother, whom his father came out and entreated, apparently in vain.

The differences which we have now to observe are of another type. The most important of them may be classified under (1) increased variety of motives and of standards suggested, (2) further analysis of the positive qualities of Christian character, and (3) a new emphasis on the sins of strife and party-spirit and also on the evil of sexual immorality. If we regard these, as I think we must, as developments harmonising with Christian experience and reflecting especially the problems of the Christian community, they serve to emphasise the early character of the teaching of the Gospels. In other words, it is difficult to believe as Kundsin[1] and others would have us do, that most of the ethical teaching of the Gospels had its origin in the community and is contemporary with Paul's Epistles. Some of it no doubt had; but of much that was seriously concerning the Church when the Epistles were written there is no trace in the Gospels.

St Paul makes great use of the appeal to reason as providing for the Christian a motive for ethical effort and achievement. It is here that we see evidence of the interlocking of religion and

[1] Kundsin, *Das Urchristentum im Lichte der Evangelienforschung*, 1929.

morality. Indirectly also we find striking witness to his conviction as to the effective reality of the Christian experience. "If"—as is surely the case —"ye then be risen with Christ, seek those things which are above" (Col. iii. 1). "If"—as is surely the case—"we are alive by the Spirit, by the Spirit let us conduct ourselves" (Gal. v. 25). His appeal to Philemon is practically this, "If you are really a child of God, treat Onesimus as a brother, for he is one too". This kind of appeal to reason, to the desire for consistency of thought which is natural to a reasonable man, provides the basis for a summons both to active goodness and to the stern suppression of evil. "Ye were once darkness, but are now light in the Lord.... The fruit of the light is in all manner of goodness and righteousness and truth" (Eph. v. 8, 9). On the other hand, "Ye are dead, and your life is hid with Christ in God ...slay therefore those members that belong to earth, immorality, base passion, evil desire and grasping greed. Strip off all these things, anger, rage, malice, abusive speech, foul talk" (Col. iii. 3, 5, 8)—a passage in which Paul, consciously or unconsciously, reproduces the idiom of our Lord's language about the members which cause to stumble as well as some of His teaching as to what defiles a man. And it is a striking fact that in all the various communities which he addresses he not only uses the same form of appeal, but evidently feels himself justified in presuming that the same spiritual experiences are common to them all and common in them all, and expressed in the same or synonymous terms. Paul is convinced that the experience of salvation of life on a higher plane is real; and that being so, it will be only natural to care for the things which belong to the higher life and to shun those which belong to the lower. A special case of this reasoning occurs when the new experience is expressed in terms of personal relation to Christ. To that we shall return later.

St Paul does not shrink from basing his ethical appeal upon solemn warnings as to the consequences of disobedience, as he would say, to the Spirit, "They which do such things shall not inherit the kingdom of God" (Gal. v. 21), teaching which had already entered into his Mission-preaching in Galatia.

And what were the works of the flesh, indulgence in which wrought this hopeless exclusion? As we examine the familiar list in Galatians and compare with it the similar list in Colossians which I have quoted, we are struck, in the first place, with the correspondence between this and the teaching of Jesus. There is the same combination, I had almost said 'jumble', of such acts or dispositions as the law of Moses had branded, and the common Christian conscience of to-day now brands, as sin, with acts and dispositions against which, in ourselves at least, we direct the mildest criticism. There are the "grosser sins", sexual immorality, impurity, debauchery, which all moralists would condemn, drinking bouts and drunken revelry, which most decent people would condemn, idolatry and the use of magic potions, which we should condemn if and where they were a serious menace to religious or social life. But embedded in this list we find a new group including hatred, fanaticism[1] and furious anger, also division, and the making of parties or factions. These take the place occupied in the list given by Jesus by what injures the happiness or dignity of the individual, and they obviously introduce a new feature, namely, what injures the well-being or happiness of the community, while guarding against the same danger to individual happiness under new forms ($\check{\epsilon}\chi\theta\rho\alpha\iota$, $\zeta\tilde{\eta}\lambda o\varsigma$, $\theta\nu\mu o\acute{\iota}$). We find in Paul many other catalogues of habits of thought and conduct which he warns his converts to shun.[2]

An examination of these will bring the same characteristics to light. The emphasis is upon sin of two different types, the vice which degrades or deteriorates the personality of the sinner, and the

---

[1] So I should translate $\zeta\tilde{\eta}\lambda o\varsigma$, especially in view of the description of it given by Hesiod, "A spirit of striving among miserable men, a spirit ugly-voiced, glad of evil, with hateful eyes". See Gilbert Murray, *Rise of Greek Epic*, p. 79.

[2] E.g. Ro. xiii. 13; 1 Cor. v. 10, 11; vi. 9, 10; 2 Cor. xii. 20; Eph. iv. 31; v. 3; Col. iii. 5, 8.

sin which injures or embitters human society. There is no suggestion of sin which is primarily a wrong done to God. It is wrong which a man commits against himself, made as he is "in the image of God", or against the group to which he belongs, the family or the ἐκκλησία, to which God gives the character of sin. It becomes something in which He is concerned, something in regard to which the offender has to deal with God.

Against all such conduct St Paul warns Christians as inconsistent with the experience which is theirs in Christ, as incurring the wrath of God and as involving the forfeiture of entrance into the Kingdom.

Another motive which was certainly present, though its influence and effect are difficult to estimate, was what is described as the eschatological, the belief that the time was short, the time within which human life under its present conditions would be lived at all. For, "Maranatha", "the Lord is at hand", was a Christian watchword. And His coming would mean the final judgment of human destinies and the cessation of all relationship to the world that now is. It would be only natural that such an expectation so strongly felt should affect the ethical outlook in more ways than one. It might well give a temporary character to all regulations affecting social life, and encourage ethical demands which though reasonable for a

brief interval of weeks or months would be unreasonable or impossible for a period measured by
a life-time or by centuries. It is curious therefore
that there is so little trace of this motive as affecting
the specific ethical teaching of St Paul.[1] It appears
indeed only in connection with his teaching about
marriage (1 Cor. vii. 26–28). And even there we
find no suggestion that marriage is anything un-
becoming in those who anticipate the early return
of the Lord. It is in view of the impending distress,
the tribulation which is to precede the coming, that
he urges unmarried people to remain as they are.
"I seek to spare you." Otherwise, the eschatological motive is appealed to as the ground for a
general attitude to life, an attitude of soberness,
self-discipline and seriousness, as of those who
watch for their Lord (1 Thess. v. 4–7). The same
effect is looked for from the same motive in
1 Peter (iv. 7; cp. i. 13; v. 8). "The end of all
things is at hand. Be self-possessed and serious
unto prayer. Above all, keep *alert your love to* one
another." If Paul proceeds in the Corinthian passage (1. vii. 29–31) to illustrate the attitude which
he would have Christians take up to the world,
we shall not insist on taking him literally any more
than we insist on always understanding his Master
literally. "The time is short" (literally, "has been

[1] See von Dobschütz, "Motives for Behaviour by the Early
Christians" in *American Journal of Theology*, xv. 505.

narrowed"). "It remains therefore that even
those who have wives should be as those who have
not,...And those who buy as those who do not
possess, and those who use the external things of
life as those who are not absorbed in them."[1]
For the outward frame of things is temporary. Do
we not catch echoes of our Lord's teaching especially in the reference to property? And is not the
general attitude here described such as is reflected
in all parts of the New Testament? A paradoxical
attitude, if you like, but one which necessarily
follows from the paradoxical character of the end,
always impending but not immediate, "In an
hour that ye know not", but even when the signs
of the times appear most ominous, "the end is not
yet". The sky becomes "blank again, At the chance
of his appearance failing". Meanwhile, the busi-
ness of the Christian is, if I may use the phrase,
to "sit loose to the world". He is in the world,
but not of the world. He is not called upon to
'renounce' the world, neither is he permitted to
assert it, or allow it to assert its power over him.
He is free. But it is with the freedom of one for
whom the world has lost both its terrors and its
glamour, who uses it as the outward and temporary
framework of a life which is "hid with Christ in
God".

A third motive of which Paul makes considerable

---

[1] Joh. Weiss, *ad loc.* "sich hingeben".

use may perhaps be described as corporate interest, the affectionate interest in the Ecclesia or
Christian community and in each of its members,
which he takes for granted in every Christian.
Paul does not expressly bid men love the Church,
though he proclaims that Christ loves the Church.
But, if he leaves that to Peter (1. ii. 16), he every-
where assumes such love as a motive. This and
several other points in Paul's method as a student
and a teacher of ethics are well illustrated in
Eph. iv. 20 ff. The first point is the interlocking of
three things which men are all too apt to hold
apart—worship, doctrine and conduct. Paul begins
(v. 20) by alluding to worship. "Ye have not so
learned Christ; if so be that ye have heard him,
and been taught in him." There is of course no
suggestion that people at Ephesus had heard the
voice of Christ even in a metaphorical or spiritual
sense. The grammar is against that. Paul means
that they had heard the whole message about
Jesus, the Gospel. But when he says "and been
taught in him" he refers to worship. For 'in
Christ' is equivalent to 'in the Fellowship', in the
Ecclesia assembled for worship. There they were
taught, there they learnt. They discovered truth.
What Paul refers to here as the truth discovered is
the possibility and necessity of being renewed in
the spirit of their mind, having put off the old man
and put on the new—as in reality Jesus Himself

had done ($\kappa\alpha\theta\dot{\omega}\varsigma$ $\dot{\epsilon}\sigma\tau\iota\nu$ $\dot{\alpha}\lambda\eta\theta\epsilon\dot{\iota}\alpha$ $\dot{\epsilon}\nu$ $\tau\hat{\omega}$ $\dot{I}\eta\sigma o\hat{v}$, cp. 2 Cor. vii. 14). But this truth or doctrine is immediately followed by, and connected with, very practical ethical teaching. "Wherefore, lie not one to another; let no corrupt communication proceed out of your mouth." The whole passage is obviously an instructive expansion of Ro. xii. 2. The Fellowship is the organ of insight.[1] The love or *Agapé* which is there generated and comes to expression is the atmosphere wherein Christian knowledge advances. It is $\sigma\dot{v}\nu$ $\pi\hat{\alpha}\sigma\iota\nu$ $\tau o\hat{\iota}\varsigma$ $\dot{\alpha}\gamma\dot{\iota}o\iota\varsigma$, in the company of all God's people, that men are to grasp the depth and breadth and height of the love of Christ (Eph. iii. 19).

But what specially concerns us here is the kind of motive which Paul attaches to these precepts: "Lie not one to another, seeing that ye are members one of another". Let the pilferer ($\dot{o}$ $\kappa\lambda\dot{\epsilon}\pi\tau\omega\nu$), the slacker who saves himself half a day's labour by what he picks off the market stalls, do a good day's work "that he may have to give to him that needeth". The man of a loose tongue is to curb his habit of corrupting speech, and substitute for what breaks down the moral fibre speech that "is good, turning the occasion to edifying", that is to say, upbuilding. In every case the motive appealed to is the controlling interest which each Christian is understood to have in the community and its

[1] See *The Spirit*, ed. Canon Streeter, pp. 145 f.

members. And only the unfortunate use of the word 'edification' for οἰκοδομή by our translators obscures from the English reader the evidence that Paul counted on love of the Church and desire for its growth internal and external as a potent force in the Christian character.

A fourth motive on which Paul bases his ethical appeal is specially important. In Ro. xii. 2 he analyses the Will of God into "the Good, the Well-pleasing and the Ideal". And the second of these factors calls attention to the ambition to please God as one of the strongest motives for ethical effort and achievement. It was not only that Paul in his preaching sought to please not men but God (1 Thess. ii. 4), but he had made it part of his preaching to urge men to behave so that they pleased God (1 Thess. iv. 1). "Wherefore", he says in 2 Corinthians (v. 9), "we make it our ambition to please him". He bids the Ephesians (v. 8) "behave as children of light...ascertaining what is well-pleasing to God" (cp. Col. iii. 20; Heb. xii. 28). "They that are in the flesh cannot please God" (Ro. viii. 8).

It cannot be claimed that this motive appears in Christian ethics only. It plays no inconsiderable part in the teaching of Epictetus. But there is this important difference, that in the Pauline teaching it forms part of the whole religious-ethical system. The God Whom the Christians seek to please is

One Who is known to them ("in the face or person of Jesus Christ") as "the gods" were not known to Epictetus. And He is known as Father, while they know themselves as sons (1 John iii. 1). The moral ambition springs out of a personal relationship already established. On the other hand, this motive differs fundamentally from that which springs out of the contractual relationship of Jewish legalism. In other words, Paul has seized not only the fact that Christians have entered upon an entirely new footing with God, the footing of His loyal children instead of servants for hire or by compulsion; he has seized also the ethical value of the fact. And as the goal of conformity to the ideal set forth by Jesus in the Sermon on the Mount is "that ye may become sons of your Father in heaven", so what Paul looks forward to as the goal of ethical development is "the revelation of the sons of God" (Ro. viii. 19). Thus the development which began in a personal relation to God, and proceeded as an ambition to please Him as Father, obtained a cosmic significance inasmuch as when complete it would satisfy "the eager expectation of all created being".

The ethical motives on which Paul relies and to which he makes appeal are much more important than even the ethical regulations or ideals which he sets forth; for it is in them, and in the ethical standards which we must now consider, that his system, if we must call it so, finds first its dynamic and then its norm. It is also in the motives, and in the standards, much more than in the detailed precepts, that we are to find what is original in his teaching when compared either with that of Judaism on the one hand or with the ethical teachers of Greece on the other. It is exceedingly interesting to take such "catalogues of vices" or "lists of virtues" as Lietzmann and others have called attention to, and compare the contents with similar lists which may be constructed from the writings of St Paul. And one who comes fresh to the study of contemporary ethics will not improbably be surprised to discover how much the Christian and the non-Christian systems have in common both in the virtues they praise and in the vices they denounce.[1] And the first result in those who concentrate attention on these details is apt to be the conclusion either that there is little or nothing that is strictly original in Paul or that measured by the standard of philosophical ethics his system shows no clear superiority over the others.

I could imagine that Paul himself would be very little disturbed by such discoveries. He was prepared to take ethical suggestions wherever he found them, in Moses or later Judaism, in Epicurus

[1] A readily accessible and admirable introduction to this study is provided by Bp Lightfoot's essay of "St Paul and Seneca" in his commentary on *Philippians*.

or Zeno, in the moral atmosphere of his time, and having tested them in the light of Christian motives and standards to "hold fast that which was good". And as for the authority with which his teaching may come home to men now, that is only increased by the fact that so much of that teaching in detail confirms or is confirmed by men of great intellectual power who gave themselves to the study of good life, in what it consists. Paul's great desire was to get things done. His great conviction is that he and his fellow-Christians possess in the Gospel something which is "a Divine Force unto salvation". And salvation while it means freedom, freedom from fear, from condemnation, from every kind of moral servitude including servitude to sin, means the power to discover what is the will of God and the power to do it.

Lecture V

THE APOSTLE: ILLUSTRATIONS
OF HIS ETHICAL PRINCIPLES

THE standards of Christian living which Paul set before his converts may be classified under three different types, according as they take the form of law, of example, or of the intuition of the educated conscience. As we have already seen, Paul was very far from looking on the moral law of the Ten Commandments as abrogated by or in Christ (cp. Col. iii. 20; Eph. vi. 1, 3). The ceremonial law he seems to have regarded as irrelevant, though even "circumcision has its value". He held still that the Jews had in their law "the embodiment of knowledge and truth" (Ro. ii. 20; cp. 1 Cor. vii. 19), and he assumes throughout the continued validity of the prohibitions against idolatry, murder, theft, adultery and covetousness. There are cases, though not many, where he appeals to the words of Jesus, and many more where we cannot but feel that he is reproducing in his own way the ethical teaching of our Lord. A second type of standard which he sets up is example, the example of himself or of Christ, or even of God. "Be ye imitators of me, as I also am of Christ" (1 Cor. xi. 1). Here he seems to invite a general imitation, not merely imitation in a specific line of conduct (cp. Phil. iv. 9); on the other hand, in 1 Thess. ii. 7–9 he invites specific imitation of his own life of industry and toil. In one passage he boldly calls on Christians to be "imitators of God, as beloved children" (Eph. v. 1), though the context appears to define the field wherein the imitation is to be practised— "forgiving one another as God in Christ forgave you", and "walk in love". The example of Christ is more freely appealed to (Ro. xv. 7; Eph. v. 2, 25, 29; Col. iii. 13; 1 Thess. i. 6). And alongside the formula ἐν Χριστῷ we find the significant phrase κατὰ Χριστόν as a norm of Christian conduct. "May God grant you to be in harmony with one another *in Christ's way*" (Ro. xv. 5; cp. 2 Cor. xi. 17; Col. ii. 8). "Welcome one another as Christ also welcomed you" (Ro. xv. 7) calls on Christians to translate their experience of Christ into conduct towards other men. And in Phil. ii. 5 the appeal to "consider not your own interests, but the interests of others" is supported by the summons to "have the same mind which was also in Christ", to take His point of view. It is then not merely the external example of Jesus which Paul set up as an ethical guide, but the ideal life and attitude to God and man which is manifested in all that is known of Him.

We must not, however, overlook a third type of

ethical standard, what I have called the intuitions of an educated conscience. Christians are to behave in a way worthy of God (1 Thess. ii. 12), in a way worthy of the Lord unto all well-pleasing (Col. i. 10), in a way worthy of their calling (Eph. iv. 1) or of the Gospel of Christ (Phil. i. 27). They are to welcome a sister in a way worthy of God's people (Ro. xvi. 2). As one ponders these sentences, the phrase which comes into one's mind is *noblesse oblige*. In the best sense of the word these people were a spiritual aristocracy. Part of Macaulay's description of the Puritans might be applied with even better right to them. "They esteemed themselves rich in a more precious treasure...nobles by the right of an earlier creation, and priests by the imposition of a mightier hand." Remember the Apostle's words to the Corinthians (1. iv. 8), "Have you entered into kingship apart from us? I would you had indeed done so, that I and you might be kings together". Or those of St Peter (1. ii. 9), "Ye are a chosen people, a royal body". Or, to take a different aspect of the status of Christians, we have St John—"Behold what manner of love the Father hath bestowed upon us, that we should be called children of God: *and such we are*" (1 John iii. 1).

That was the *noblesse*, and much of Paul's ethical teaching represents the working out of the obligation that attaches to it. Thus, he expects his

converts to behave with decorum, εὐσχημόνως (Ro.
xiii. 13) and particularly towards outsiders (1 Thess.
iv. 12; cp. 1 Cor. xiv. 40). The word is one for which
it is difficult to find an equivalent in English. The
context in Romans suggests that it is specially anything that would cause public scandal, which is to
be avoided. As Benjamin Jowett says, "It is characteristic of St Paul to ask, What will the Gentiles
say of us?, a part of the Christian prudence which
was one of the great features of his life".[1] Better,
perhaps, remembering ἀξίως, What will they say
of our Lord and of His Gospel?[2]

It is practically the same standard to which the
Apostle refers when he repudiates in general τὰ
μὴ καθήκοντα (Ro. i. 28) or τὰ οὐκ ἀνήκοντα (Eph.
v. 4). He meant that there were many kinds of
thought and action, which, even if there was no
law against them, were morally disgusting and
therefore impossible for the Christian. On the
other hand, Paul left it to Philemon to discover
what was 'fitting' (τὸ ἀνῆκον) as to his future
relation with Onesimus. That is to say, he trusted
the educated Christian conscience to ascertain
what was the will of God. And he believed that
the education of conscience went on largely within
the Fellowship and was mediated through its
worship.

[1] *Cit.* Milligan *ad* 1 Thess. iv. 12.
[2] Cp. 2 Cor. viii. 21.

Another standard belonging to the same type is contained in the idea suggested by συμφέρει, τὸ συμφέρον.[1] Here also St Paul adopts a criterion which was already current in Greek ethical teaching.[2] We find a useful definition of its meaning in Seneca, "quidquid nos meliores beatosque facturum". It offers therefore as a criterion of conduct for the Christian, and indeed the most important internal one, the question whether by this or that action he will be serving the true advantage either of himself or of others. It presupposes therefore the acceptance by the Christian of another purpose in life than self-pleasing or the assertion of his rights or even of his liberty. Paul uses the idea in two passages which show the important place which it occupies in his ethical system. According to the Authorised Version they run, "All things are lawful for me, but all things are not expedient" (1 Cor. vi. 12; x. 23), where the word 'expedient' is obviously most unfortunate. It suggests to the modern reader a standard below the moral one, one of calculating self-interest. 'Advantageous' has been suggested; but that is

---

[1] This is practically the same principle as that which has been discussed as a motive under 'corporate interest'. Only it applies to the ethical problems of the Christian as an individual no less than as a member of society; and it functions as a standard no less than as a motive.

[2] See illustrations collected by Joh. Weiss, *Erster Korintherbrief*, p. 158 n.

open to the same ambiguity. We may at least para-
phrase thus: "All things are permissible to me; but
not all things are serviceable" to the nobler life.
The first clause (πάντα μοι ἔξεστιν) may have
been used by St Paul; it would be a natural expression of his joyful consciousness of freedom from
the Law. But they are not his own words here.
They are quoted by him from some persons at
Corinth who have thrown them back at him,
having, perhaps wilfully, misunderstood him.
These persons are now claiming his authority to
ignore all moral obligations. Paul does not recoil
from the position. He quotes their words, but
cancels their inference by adding ἀλλ' οὐ πάντα
συμφέρει. This is indeed the safeguard against
Antinomianism, the principle which makes liberty
incompatible with licence. The licence or freedom
from all moral restraint which these people are
claiming is not true freedom at all. It is a new
bondage, a bondage to the lusts of the flesh. "And
I", says St Paul, "am not going to let anything
master me." "Ye have been called unto freedom;
only use not freedom as an opportunity for the
flesh, but by love serve one another" (Gal. v. 13).
Love is to prompt the voluntary subordination of
freedom, priceless gift as it is, to the moral and
religious well-being of others.

A consideration of these standards makes it
clear that St Paul conceived of the Christian as

having in ethical matters a free judgment which moved within certain wide frontiers defined by the revealed will of God, and at the same time was continuously inspired by high example and guided by a delicate perception of what was "worthy of the Lord", what was becoming in His followers, what was for the good of the Church and what was seemly in the eyes of men. These things were elements in that will of God for which the spiritual man had an instinctive perception, but an even surer and clearer perception when he was "in the Fellowship of God's people".

We could not have a better illustration of Paul's application of the Christian motives to a difficult problem of conduct than his handling of the question of the "weaker brethren" or "those who are weak in the faith" in Romans xiv. By "weak in the faith" he does not mean "unsound in the essentials" or even wavering in their personal trust in Jesus Christ. He is using 'faith' in the sense of 'conviction'. And the persons to whom he is referring are those whose conviction as to the irrelevance of the ritual regulations to which they had submitted in the past is not sufficiently strong to prevent them from still observing them, on the principle of 'safety first', or to prevent them from being shocked when they saw other Christians ignoring them. The regulations in question had largely to do with food. There were certain kinds of meat of which the Jew was strictly forbidden to partake. Such meats were 'unclean' and rendered him who partook of them 'unclean'. He was disqualified for attendance at the sanctuary. It was true that Jesus had "cleansed all meats" (Mk. vii. 19), and Paul was convinced that "there is nothing unclean of itself". But there were some Christians who could not overcome the ingrained habit of thought. And Paul shows his psychological insight when he says of such "to him who reckons anything unclean, it is unclean". It gives him an uneasy conscience. He is not free to partake of it himself, and if he sees his fellow-Christians partaking freely of what is forbidden by the Law, he experiences a shock which may ruin his faith. And as that might happen at any common meal, it raised a question which was serious for the unity and peace of each body of believers.

How does Paul deal with it? In the first place he urges those whose grasp on spiritual realities is strong to welcome the weak, though not to contentious discussions. Then he points out the duty of each party. The one who feels free to eat anything is not to despise him who abstains; neither is he who abstains to criticise him who claims entire freedom in such matters. The important fact is that both alike have received the welcome of God.

The second illustration of such unnecessary

scruples is taken from the superstitious observance of special days (Ro. xiv. 5). The reference may be to Jewish festivals, the weekly Sabbath, the new moons, the annual Feasts, the Sabbath itself having become an object of superstitious reverence, which turned it into a burden and a snare. Or, Paul may have had in mind Gentile forms of superstition according to which certain days or dates were connected with certain of the planets, or the elemental forces that ruled the world (Gal. iv. 9, 10), and men shaped their conduct on these days accordingly.[1] In this case the same rule applied. Each man must be "fully persuaded in his own mind". Each man was to be held fully responsible for his own conviction and the application he gave to it. These were not matters on which it was necessary that the whole community should think or act alike. Paul's conviction was that if men could but realise clearly and continuously their relation in Christ, these problems would solve themselves. The truth is, no one of us Christians is an isolated individual (Ro. xiv. 7). For Christians to criticise one another in matters such as these is to take up an attitude of independence towards one another which is incompatible with their common

[1] See F. H. Colson, *The Week*, p. 8, "The plain man believed vaguely but profoundly in the power of the planets. He rose on Friday or Saturday with the belief that those days were somehow under the influence, the one of the beneficent, the other of the maleficent star".

life in and for Christ. And further it is inconsistent with the humility which becomes those who must all appear before the judgment-seat of Christ. The sum of the matter is that to those who are strong in the faith Paul appeals that they should not give the cold shoulder to the weak, but give them a place of welcome in the Fellowship, showing patience and toleration; to the weak and over-scrupulous he appeals with even more elabora-tion of argument that they should refrain from criticising those who claim to exercise freedom in matters of external observance.

In the next paragraph (*vv.* 13–23) the Apostle turns again to those whose faith-conviction is strong enough to set them free from scruples and from self-imposed asceticism, and urges them to take a further step and for love's sake waive the exercise of their right to freedom. If by the osten-tatious use of food, meat or drink, which your brother in Christ thinks to be forbidden, you cause him pain and distress of conscience, then it is not love that guides your conduct. Do nothing to bring disaster on your brother, "for whom Christ died". Do not, merely to gratify your own taste or appetite, undermine the work of God (*v.* 19). You are rightly thankful for your greater enlighten-ment; but keep it as something between you and God. Remember that even if your brother is led by your example to partake when he is not sure that he is not doing wrong, you are doing him an injury. For he that eats, not feeling certain that it is right, has been condemned already.[1]

Further illustration of Paul's application of the same principle is found in his handling of the question of meats offered to idols in 1 Cor. viii. And as we study these passages we receive an almost startling impression of the identity of these principles with those which we have found underlying the ethical teaching of Jesus. There is the same recognition, in Paul's case triumphant recognition, of the rights, especially the right to self-determination (Lk. xii. 57) and freedom from ritual regulations, which have been conferred on the Christian by God in Christ. There is the same sharp criticism of those who would seek to use human tradition in order to bring men into moral servitude (Mk. vii. 13, "invalidating the word of God by your tradition"; Col. ii. 8, κατὰ τὴν παράδοσιν τῶν ἀνθρώπων). As Jesus illustrates His point by a reference to the Jewish practice of Corban, so Paul makes plain what he means by referring to the watchword of the false asceticism, "Touch not, taste not, handle not", and urges the Colossians not to allow themselves to be browbeaten by such maxims. The independence, the

[1] For a fuller exposition of this important passage I may refer to my commentary on the *Epistle to the Romans* in the *Abingdon Commentary*.

freedom and the dignity which mark the status of the Christian, to these the teaching of Jesus and of Paul alike bear witness. But—there is the same insistence on the duty of waiving these rights, of yielding a voluntary subordination to the interests, especially the moral and spiritual interests, of others. There is the same emphasis on the anxious care necessary to avoid putting a stumbling-block in another's way (Ro. xiv. 21; 1 Cor. viii. 13), the same warning against the critical temper of superiority (Mt. vii. 1–5; Ro. xiv. 4). And at the base of it all there is the same appeal to *Agapé*. What makes reasonable the invitation to humility, subordination of self, waiving of personal rights, is the basal fact that Christians are bound to one another by the love "which gives cohesion to the perfect life" (ὅ ἐστιν σύνδεσμος τῆς τελειότητος, Col. iii. 14).

What we see is St Paul applying these principles of Jesus, and doing it with extraordinary firmness and precision, to new situations, such as are not directly contemplated in the teaching of our Lord. And that is not only because the particular problems had not arisen, but because the community that produced them was not yet in being. Again I ask myself whether the ethical teaching in the Gospels does not as a whole reflect an historical situation anterior to the coming into existence of "the churches of God in Christ Jesus".

My purpose, as I have said at the beginning of these lectures, is not so much to expound in detail the ethical teaching of the New Testament, in the various aspects of Christian duty and relationship,[1] as to try to discover the guiding principles which underlie the teaching. Some of these principles are enshrined or crystallised in Paul's vocabulary. And I propose now to consider two or three of the pregnant words of this type, encouraged in the task by the striking saying of the late Sir Walter Raleigh; "life is spent in learning the meaning of great *words* so that some idle proverb, known for a lifetime, comes home on a day like a blow".

Take first the common word ἀλήθεια. The commentators have long recognised that there are not a few passages in the New Testament in which this word is not adequately rendered by 'truth' in the sense of what is consonant with fact or of a proposition which forms an integral part of a total revelation. In the prologue of St John's Gospel, for example, and the familiar phrase, "We beheld his glory full of grace and truth", it is commonly rendered by *Treue*, loyalty or sincerity. Walter Bauer goes further and paraphrases, "a perfect instrument of Divine revelation". To me it appears to go yet deeper, and to describe a deep-lying quality or characteristic, the power of perceiving reality. Its effects are manifested both ethically

[1] For an examination of these I may refer to my *Christianity according to St Paul*, pp. 221 ff.

(sincerity) and intellectually (truth). I have noted certain passages in which St Paul uses the word in a very significant way. Take three of these—Eph. iv. 24 ἐν ὁσιότητι τῆς ἀληθείας (the rendering of A.V., "in true holiness", is obviously unsatisfactory); 2 Thess. ii. 10, τὴν ἀγάπην τῆς ἀληθείας; ii. 13, ἐν πίστει ἀληθείας.[1] The genitive in each of these cases is a genitive of origin, describing that from which something starts or by which it is started. It is dynamic rather than static. And we may compare the saying, "Ye shall know the truth, and the truth shall make you free" (John viii. 32). We shall probably get nearest to Paul's meaning in such cases if we take as the modern equivalent of ἀλήθεια "reality revealed or recognised", or "reality as revealed in Jesus Christ". If so, the promise in the fourth Gospel that the Spirit will lead the Church "into all truth" takes on a new meaning. It is what Jesus did partially, at least, for His disciples. And we may trust His Spirit to do the same and more for the Church.

Another word of the same type but of a different class is πλεονεξία. I observe that von Dobschütz commits himself to the strange opinion that this is a 'colourless' word, whereas to me it seems to be one of the most colourful words in Paul's ethical vocabulary. In our Authorised Version it is translated eight times by 'covetousness', once by 'greediness'; the corresponding substantive by

[1] Cp. 1 Pet. i. 22 and Hort's note.

'covetous man', and the corresponding verb once by 'defraud' and once by 'overreach'. But 'covetous' is quite inadequate as a rendering, suggesting as it does, at least to a modern reader, almost exclusively the coveting of money and property, that is, avarice. In one case R.V. renders 'extortion'. But some meaning nearer to the etymology of the word seems to be called for. It is, as Trench says, the temper that seeks to grasp what it has not, and in this way to have more, the *amor sceleratus habendi*. Cowley in his essay on Avarice has drawn the distinction well. "There are two sorts of avarice; the one is but of a bastard kind, and that is the rapacious appetite for gain; not for its own sake but for the pleasure of refunding it through all the channels of pride and luxury; the other is the true kind, and properly so called, which is a restless and unsatiable desire of riches, not for any further end or use, but only to hoard and preserve. The covetous man of the first kind is like a greedy ostrich, which devours any metal, but it is with intent to feed upon it, and, in effect, it makes shift to digest it. The second is like a foolish chough which loves to steal money only to hide it." Πλεονεξία therefore is the drawing and snatching to himself, on the sinner's part, of the creature in every form and kind.[1]

[1] See Trench, *Synonyms of the New Testament*, pp. 94 ff., from which these quotations are taken.

If we must find a single word for πλεονεξία then, we must take such a one as 'possessiveness' used by the psychologists, or 'acquisitiveness' with which Mr Tawney has made us familiar, though on the whole the best seems to me to be 'insatiableness'.

It is important to remember that it is included in our Lord's list of the things that defile a man, where it stands between adultery and maliciousness (Mk. vii. 22; cf. Lk. xii. 15). Paul classes it with πονηρία (Ro. i. 29), and in 1 Corinthians places the insatiable between thieves and drunkards. But the deep significance he gives to the word is seen in Col. iii. 5, and in Eph. iv. 19 (cp. 1 Cor. v. 10; Eph. v. 3, 5). In the Colossian passage he identifies πλεονεξία with idolatry (πλεονεξία ἥτις ἐστὶν εἰδωλολατρεία), and shows thereby his perception that idolatry is by no means confined to bowing down to stocks and stones or graven images of any kind, but includes any kind of absorption and exclusive trust in the material things of life. Πλεονεξία, 'insatiableness', means, in the ultimate issue, the final exclusion of all spiritual values.

St Paul recognises a second significant manifestation of *pleonexia* in sexual immorality. It seems probable that Trench went too far when he spoke of the Apostle as identifying *pleonexia* with impurity in the same way as he identifies it with idolatry.

But he does so frequently bring the two into close juxtaposition that the impression becomes very strong that he feels the one to be a manifestation of the other.[1] And such indeed it is seen to be, especially in extreme cases where not only is no limit set to the number of victims, but the gratification of self seems to find its culmination in the ruthless exercise of power over another personality. Immorality is therefore the extreme form of *pleonexia*, what Cicero calls *libido inexplebilis*, what Shakespeare has described as

> The cloyed will,
> That satiate yet unsatisfied desire,
> That tub both filled and running.[2]

1. On this subject the first thing to observe is that Paul makes it clear in his first Epistle to the Thessalonians that already in his Mission Preaching at Thessalonica he had dealt fully and faithfully with the duty of sexual purity. It may be difficult for other reasons to accept the traditional view that all the Apostle's work at Thessalonica was accomplished in three weeks or so. But not much longer can be allowed for his sojourn there, and it is very significant that he found time and made opportunity to enforce this teaching on the consciences

---

[1] E.g. 1 Cor. v. 11; vi. 9; Eph. iv. 19; v. 3; compare also 1 Thess. iv. 6, where he uses πλεονεκτεῖν as a periphrasis for adultery.

[2] *Cymbeline*, Act 1, Sc. 6; *cit*. Trench, who has an admirable study of this word.

of his converts. Dibelius has given it as his opinion
that we must assume that he followed the same
course whenever he broke new ground. So far is it
from being true, that his Mission Preaching was
confined within the limits suggested by the verse
in 1 Corinthians, "I determined to know nothing
among you, save Jesus Christ, and him crucified".

2. Paul here challenged the very citadel of
human selfishness and self-assertion against God.
How far and with what effect it had been challenged before is extremely difficult to say. Probably he had some support from Judaism; almost
certainly he had none from the public opinion or
even from the recognised moralists of the Hellenic
world. The Mosaic legislation had of course placed
its ban upon adultery, and had been followed
therein both by the public opinion and by the
legislation of Greece and Rome. And we have been
in the habit of extending the prohibition in the
seventh commandment to include sexual irregularities of any kind—a course which may be
morally, but is not historically, justified. For even
in the Mosaic legislation, adultery is probably
looked on rather as an invasion of another's property than as a breach of sexual morality. The
witness of the Jewish literature is ambiguous.
References in the historical books would lead us to
think that πορνεία was looked on with a certain
tolerance. The strange and to us ugly story of

Judah and Tamar is related for the credit of the
woman's cleverness, and suggests no criticism of
the conduct of either of them. In or after the
Exile we find in the Book of Proverbs much wise
and impressive teaching. But the sanctions there
appealed to are prudential. The consequences
attached to lax conduct are physical. There is no
suggestion that πορνεία is a heinous sin. In the
Testaments of the Twelve Patriarchs, where the subject
is fully dealt with in the *Testament of Judah*, it is
handled with a certain half-heartedness as though
πορνεία were discreditable indeed but hardly
reckoned as sin. In the *Testament of Reuben* (iv. 6)
we find it treated more gravely. "A pit unto the
soul is the sin of πορνεία, separating from God."
But the following sentences trail off into platitudes.
On the other hand, the protests against polygamy
raised by the Essenes and by the Damascus Dissenters are clear indications of an awakening conscience on the subject. And the probability is that
by the time when Paul was writing the Jews were
both proclaiming and exhibiting a higher standard
of sexual morality.[1]

On the other hand, in the heathen world to
which Paul turned with his Gospel, vice flourished
unchecked by either conscience or public opinion.
The evidence may be found in von Dobschütz,

[1] The earliest official injunction against πορνεία appears to be
that recorded in Acts xv, the decrees of the Council at Jerusalem.

Christian Life in the Primitive Church,[1] or as summarised by Mr W. H. S. Jones.[2] "The virtue of chastity was confined within narrow limits, such as loyalty to the husband on the part of the wife. Men were under no obligations, except that of avoiding adultery or dishonour to a neighbour's family. It is hard to find a passage in pre-Christian Greek literature where loose intercourse is looked upon as in itself a moral offence. Sexual indulgence stood upon exactly the same moral level as eating and drinking. Philosophy made no attempt to alter this moral attitude. Even the Stoics, with their relatively ascetic morality, made no effort to combat the sensuality of the time."

3. It was accordingly a new note in ethical teaching which was struck when Jesus, as recorded in Mark vii, puts πορνεία as well as μοιχεία or adultery in the list of things which disqualify a man for fellowship with God. And there is nothing which bears more convincing testimony to Paul's confidence in Christ and in the Gospel as a Divine Force unto salvation than the fact that in the name of Christ he challenged this gigantic evil.

He set up, for the first time, so far as I can see, a standard of personal purity, and proclaimed that it was to this that God had called men (1 Thess.

[1] P. 367, etc. Compare Harnack, *Expansion of Christianity*, I. 488, and J. W. Hunkin, *JTS*, xxvii. 282.
[2] *Greek Morality*, pp. 118, 119.

iv. 7), that for this also the grace of God was sufficient. It should no longer be necessary to expose the false interpretation which till lately commentators were in the habit of putting on Paul's reiterated warnings against sensuality. They have found in them evidence of a rapid and distressing decline of morality among the Christian communities. They have found in Paul's utterances on the subject the expression of his disappointment and alarm. They would have spared themselves the mistake if they had used their imagination to realise the tremendous difficulty of the task to which Paul set himself, the physical urge combined with the social push towards every kind of immorality, the moral atmosphere impregnated with vice, the public obscenities, the theatre and the palaestra. Or, if they had taken the trouble to acquaint themselves with the situation in large parts of the Foreign Mission field to-day. There it is part of the task of our Missionaries with infinite patience and persuasiveness to expound to converts living in a similar environment the first principles of Christian morality. And that is what we find Paul doing in his letters, repeating instruction which he had already given by word of mouth, with no loss of patience, with no trace of doubt as to the power of the Gospel to meet this demand.

4. In what way or ways did St Paul bring that

power to bear? I observe that most of the books speak of chastity as "a religious virtue". If the writers mean that there are no sanctions for this virtue outside religion, they are of course mistaken. But if they mean that the strongest sanctions and perhaps the only conclusive ones are those which appeal only to the religious man, they are right. How then does Paul state these sanctions? Perhaps we shall get the answer in the briefest form if we imagine him trying to help a young convert, say one who is in danger of temptation.

Paul never shrinks from using a steam-hammer to crack a nut, bringing the most tremendous facts of Christian truth or experience to bear upon the social or moral problem of an individual. So he begins by reminding his convert that he belongs to Christ, is in fact united to Him in the bond of love which is established by faith. Is it not therefore simply preposterous and irrational that he should ever think of making himself over to "the strange woman"? (1 Cor. vi. 15). (I note in passing that Paul there finds the strongest moral appeal in the *unio mystica*.) Or look at it another way. "Your body is the temple of the Holy Spirit" (1 Cor. vi. 19). The Spirit dwells in you, and consecrates your whole personality—body, soul and spirit. Promiscuous relations involve for you so terrible an internal contradiction that nothing short of the destruction of your moral personality can follow. For you are up against the mystery of creation, the Divine purpose which is involved in it. "Male and female created he them." There is that in the original constitution of the sexes, as a result of which their coming together produces not only a physical but a psychical unit, what might be described as a new personality.

If you do not read German, you should get someone who does to translate to you pages 163 and 165 of Weiss' great Commentary on 1 Corinthians. He points to the absence in both Hebrew and Greek of any word for what we try to express by personality, and suggests that writers in these languages were compelled to use some strange substitutes. With one of them (πρόσωπον) we are familiar from the history of the Creed. Weiss finds another in σῶμα or body (apply this to 1 Cor. vi. 16), and believes that Paul put the same meaning even upon σάρξ (flesh) in the verse he quotes from Genesis, "The twain shall be one flesh", one personality. We may take it so if we please, or we may say that since Genesis was written we have been led to see that there is not only μία σάρξ (one flesh) but μία ψύχη (one soul) and ἓν πνεῦμα (one spirit). It follows that the union is one which cannot be safely regarded as transient in its character or limited in its consequences. Weiss concludes his exposition of the passage by saying, "We perceive how entirely new and previously

unthought of these arguments are; for that reason
they are not quite complete or quite free from
criticism. But Christian ethics has not yet carried
the subject much further". The writers of the ex-
cellent volume on this subject in the Copec Reports
do not seem to have been aware of it, but they
had Paul behind them when they wrote, "Physical
union between two individuals has permanent
results upon the nature of each, and therefore
should itself create a permanent relationship".
The penalty incurred by ignoring this is the dis-
integration of the personality, due to the rending
of the physical from the emotional and spiritual
elements.

But St Paul's arguments would be by no means
exhausted. In all the forms of sexual irregularity
which he is contemplating there is a victim as
well as an offender. The love thou owest to thy
neighbour absolutely closes the door to all such
conduct. And the edge of the commandment is
further sharpened, by a reminder of the sacrifice of
Christ and its consequences. Do not by the indulgence of appetite destroy that fellow-creature
for whom Christ died (Ro. xiv. 15). There is a controlling idea here which has curiously fallen into
the background of our thinking. Dr Glover has
drawn attention to the way in which it impressed
the imagination of former times. He gives a
number of illustrations. There was the Bishop in

North Africa in the fifth century who remonstrated with a Governor who was ill-treating the natives. He said, "You are treating men as if they were cheap, but man is a thing of price, for Christ died for him". There is the case quoted by Sir John Sandys of the scholar Muretus in the sixteenth century, who was journeying on foot through Italy, was picked up travel-stained and suffering on the street of a strange town. Carried to hospital and laid upon the operating table, he heard one of the doctors say to the other in Latin, "Try your experiment on this cheap life", and called out in Latin also, "Do you call a life cheap for which Christ did not disdain to die?" Again, from our own history there is John Kett when he heard those who were being tried for participation in his rebellion described as 'villeins' and called out in court, "Call not them villeins for whom Christ died". But I doubt whether this sense of the new dignity conferred on men by the sacrifice of Christ ever found finer expression than in our own *Piers Plowman*. William Langland, if he was the author, has been referring to Calvary, and then says

> Blood-brothers did we all become there
> And gentlemen each one.

Paul uses with great effect this appeal to the new dignity which has been conferred on human nature and the new brotherhood which has been established by the death of Christ. Immorality, he would argue again, is colossal selfishness, the ignoring and final denial of the freedom and the prerogatives of another personality, purchased at so great a price.

Some of these arguments may well have cogency outside the circle of those who profess loyalty to, and claim union with, Christ. But for all within that circle they would appear to have cumulative and convincing force.

St Paul saw in marriage the God-given prophylactic for all sexual irregularities (1 Cor. vii. 2, 9). It is not exactly true to say that he gave only a grudging approval to marriage. The language which seems to point that way is capable of simple explanation. For one thing we may think of him as of one who is naturally celibate, not through conscious or deliberate choice, still less in consequence of any opinion, such as afterwards came to be strongly held, that the state of virginity was morally superior to the state of marriage, but simply through entire absorption in his apostolic work. He admits, when he dissuades widows from remarrying, that he is speaking according to his own conviction (1 Cor. vii. 40), and recognises that in this matter God gives one kind of grace-gift to one man, another to another (1 Cor. vii. 7). He himself has the grace-gift of self-control. It is a question, as Weiss says, whether in the case of

really great personalities there is not sometimes an
absence of interest in married life, which is not
really a defect, but rather the symptom of a raising
of other powers and motives to an extraordinary
degree, or, as in this case, an uncommon experience
of being religiously controlled (as Paul puts it,
"apprehended by Christ"), through which whole
areas of the natural life come to be sublimated.

But even this does not prevent Paul from looking
favourably on marriage in general. Otherwise he
could never have used it as he does as a figure
to illustrate the union of Christ and the Church.
Neither would he have been at such pains to set
forth the ideals of a Christian home in the relations
between husbands and wives, between parents
and children. Conceiving and presenting these
relations, as he always does, as "in the Lord", he
holds and sets forth an ideal of family life which
is based upon marriage rightly understood and
honourably maintained. It is in the light of this
fact that certain qualifying utterances have to be
regarded. If he would have others be even as he is,
unmarried, it is partly in order that they might be
free to devote themselves without distraction to the
service of the Lord (1 Cor. vii. 35), partly because
he foresees a period of tribulation for Christians
when it will go specially hard with those who have
given hostages to fortune; "I would fain spare
you" (1 Cor. vii. 28).

Similarly, what he has to say about the status of women over against men has to be read in the light of his references to women in general which are marked by respect, appreciation and affection. "Salute Rufus—and his mother, who is a mother to me also." He acknowledges their services as freely and as fully as he acknowledges the services of men. And plainly they were services rendered within and to the Ecclesia. He even seems to reckon a woman, Junia, among the Apostles. That at least was the opinion of Chrysostom.

Again, it is in the light of these facts that we are to read the qualifications. That the verses 1 Cor. xiv. 34, 35, which close with the words, "It is disgraceful for women to speak in the church", were written by St Paul I do not believe.[1] But apart from that there are the passages where he definitely assigns a subordinate position to women. In 1 Cor. xi. 3, he says that the husband is the head of the wife; but he has just said that Christ is the head of every man, and he goes on to say that God is the head of Christ. He is obviously using the word 'head' not in the derived sense of governor, but in the natural sense, in which the head is the organ by which the body is guided. And just as the Church holds Paul's doctrine of the subordination of the Son to be not inconsistent with real equality within the Godhead, so we may recognise

[1] See *Christianity according to St Paul*, p. 227.

that the subordinate position which Paul assigns to woman is not inconsistent with spiritual equality. What he means is that in the psychological unit created by marriage, the μία σάρξ or ἐν σῶμα, the husband occupies the place of the head.

In Eph. v. 22 ff. Paul calls on wives to recognise this subordination. Unfortunately, the English reader is misled as to the character of the subordination, first by the wrong division of verses (of paragraphs in the Revised Version), then by the translation of ὑποτασσόμενοι. Restoring the connection which certainly exists between v. 21 and v. 22, we observe that what is asked of wives is the same as what has been asked of all Christians in their relation to one another. It is a mutual obligation, and if we are to apply it literally, the word cannot be rendered 'be in subjection to'. The condition described as 'subjection' is not a mutual but a one-sided one. I suppose that it is due to the Revisers' unfortunate predilection for uniformity that they have chosen 'subjection' in each of the three verses, whereas the Authorised Version has 'submit' in two cases, and 'subject' only in the third. Some may think that it is going too far in the other direction to suggest 'defer'; but I am sure that it is nearer to Paul's meaning than 'be in subjection' or even than 'submit'. In any case it prescribes for wives in relation to their husbands precisely the same attitude as is

prescribed for all Christians in relation to one
another.

I am not concerned to deny that in this matter
Paul has not entirely shaken off the estimate of
women which was universal in antiquity. It is not
entirely antiquated even now. But a just account
of all he has to say on the subject seems to me to
exonerate him from any charge of harshness or
narrow-mindedness on the subject. It is an important step, but not a very long one, which is
registered by one of the best of our modern writers
about marriage when he states the ideal of the
married state in this aspect of it, as being that
husband and wife 'alternately take the lead in their
common life".[1]

St Paul has suffered sadly at the hands of the
translators almost as much as at the hands of the
dogmatic theologians. Think of the grave results of
translating ἐφ' ᾧ in Ro. v. 12 as the Vulgate does,
"in quo omnes peccaverunt", a mistranslation
which, as Rashdall remarked, "might almost be
said to be the foundation of Augustinian theology";
or of the possibly graver results to individuals of
the translation of Ro. xiv. 23, "He that doubteth
is damned". Less serious of course but still not
without its consequences is the handling of the
word ἐπιείκεια. The 'gentleness' of Christ,
especially when it follows 'meekness' as it does in

[1] See A. H. Gray, *Man, Woman and God*, pp. 135 ff.

2 Cor. x. 1, inevitably suggests to modern ears something lacking in virility. And when our translators tried again and gave us in Phil. iv. 5, "Let your moderation be known unto all men", they put a weapon into the hands of all who in subsequent generations wished to douse enthusiasm. And we ourselves pay it but scant attention when we meet it in the New Testament. But see what trouble Aristotle took over this word, to bring out all the fullness of its meaning. "It is to pardon human failings, and to look to the law-giver and not to the law, to the spirit and not to the letter, to the intention and not to the act, to the whole and not to the part, to remember good rather than evil."[1] In the speech of Cleon in Thucydides (III. 90) it is joined with οἶκτος or compassion as one of the things most injurious to a ruling state. We have heard the same from the Cleons of our own time. It is this, however, which Paul notes as one of the characteristics of Christ (2 Cor. x. 1), and it is this which he urges Christians to display so that it may be "known unto all men" (Phil. iv. 5). And it is a striking fact that Clement of Rome (I. xiii) refers to "our Lord Jesus as teaching μακροθυμίαν καὶ ἐπιείκειαν." If we seek an illustration of this quality in His example, we may find it in the saying, "He that is not against us is on our side" (Mk. ix. 40), as well as in many matters

[1] See J. B. Mayor, *The Epistle of St James*, p. 126.

of greater moment. If we seek an illustration in
Paul we have it in the saying, "Notwithstanding
in every way, whether sincerely or insincerely,
Christ is proclaimed, and therein do I rejoice"
(Phil. i. 18), as well as in his whole attitude to life.
It is an attitude which has been caught by Brown-
ing in his description of Heracles:

> He did too many greatnesses to note
> Much in the smaller things about his path.

Doubting as I do whether any of the words which
have been suggested as rendering ἐπιείκεια are
adequate to its full meaning, I should suggest
'magnanimity'. "I beseech you by the deference
and magnanimity of Christ." "Let your magnanimity be known unto all men." This is not an
un-virile quality, far from it. Add to it ὑπομονή
which is not merely 'patience' but 'heroic en-
durance', and the whole harvest of the Spirit, a
loving heart, a cheerful disposition and a tranquil
mind; long-temperedness, good feeling and good
dealing; good faith, deference and self-control or
self-mastery, especially in the temptations of the
flesh. Here seems to be an ideal of character
balanced, complete and satisfying. And Paul
believed that it was within the reach of the
ordinary man. For it was the harvest, the natural
manifestation in human character, of the Spirit of
Christ.

Lecture VI

LIMITATIONS AND THEIR REMOVAL

I FEAR that some, perhaps many, of my hearers may be disappointed by some of the conclusions reached in the previous lectures. The natural man (and there is a survival of the natural man in every one of us) craves for external authority. He finds it hard to acquiesce in the dictum, "There shall no sign be given to it". And further we are conscious of the enormous difficulty of persuading the natural man to accept Christian standards of living except by the force of external authority. And for his sake we are tempted to discover or invent one. But the word 'tempted' may remind us that this was one of the temptations which assailed our Lord, one of the possible policies which in the wilderness He tested and rejected. And unless we are to be false to His method and disloyal to Himself we must accept His principle and follow His example. "Neither will they believe though one rise from the dead."

On the other hand, we must not forget the existence and the weight of what in the first lecture I called experimental authority, the witness of the educated Christian conscience accumulated and tested and developed through many centuries.

And this witness is specially strong and specially harmonious in the field of ethics. It is at his peril that any man either ignores or defies that authority. To insist on finding out for oneself the truth of the witness that "Whatsoever a man soweth, that shall he also reap" belongs to the same class of foolishness as insisting on testing the truth of some "law of nature" by breaking it. Of the influence of this kind of experimental authority in the field of social morality we have recently seen a striking example in the Turkish Republic. There the Government has recently prohibited polygamy, recognising at last that the isolated voices which were first raised against it (voices possibly of Essenes or of Damascus Dissenters) were right. The experience of the race has proved it. So the experience of Christendom has proved that "Whatsoever a man soweth, that shall he also reap", and much else besides.

Nevertheless, I must begin this last lecture by pointing out that the ethical teaching of the New Testament is of such a character that the effort to give it a general application to life is subject to certain definite limitations. The first limitation has to do with the area over which these ethical principles can be *expected* to operate. That area includes those and those only who have accepted Jesus as Lord, and find in the God Whom He reveals a Father, Whose will it is their ambition to discover and to obey. St Paul would put it in a more mystical way, and say, only those who are united to Christ by that faith which becomes operative through love. That is the area within which the principles of Christian ethics can be expected to operate. It does not follow that they may not or do not operate, some of them outside that area. But they operate fortuitously, sporadically, capriciously. Each man may make his own selection, and may be able through the help of heredity or environment to produce quite satisfactory results. And that is all to the good, for himself and for his world. Nevertheless, such fragmentary and auto-suggested adoption of Christian standards has only a very distant relation to Christianity, which is complete and satisfying because it represents a harmony of man's relation to the unseen world and of his relation to the world of material things. "The only thing about a human will which needs satisfying is the whole will; religion is the satisfaction of the whole will, the will to power in its inclusive form."[1] And this is what Christianity offers more simply and more perfectly than any other religion, through the interlocking of religion and morality.

This is a very important point, and I should like to consider it for a few moments. When we speak of the two as 'interlocking' we employ a useful figure, but one which is at the same time in danger

[1] W. E. Hocking, *Human Nature and its Re-making*, p. 386.

of suggesting a mechanical connection. Whereas of course the connection between religion and morality is for Christianity a vital one. They are like the two wings of an aeroplane, without either of which it would be futile to expect the plane to fly. And it is obviously foolish to charge the designer with failure if we insist on carrying out only half his design.

What gave Christianity its vitality in the first century of its existence was the sense of freedom and of power which it conveyed to men of all classes who had previously been the slaves of many shifting servitudes. And that sense came from "the knowledge of the glory of God in the person of Christ Jesus". That was the discovery of the glorious world of spirit, or of reality, which is the pure expression of the Being of God. The discovery came through the Person of Christ Jesus, through His total communication of Himself to men in words and deeds, confirmed and deepened as it had been by the Resurrection and by all subsequent experience of His spiritual presence. And the effect of this knowledge of the world of spirit or reality interpenetrating the world of material things, as what we call the ether interpenetrates the air, was to make men free, to give them a sense of power. "Ye shall know the truth (the truth of things), and the truth shall make you free." "This is the victory that overcometh the world,

even your faith", your grasp on God and on
reality. And part of the freedom, part of the
victory, was felt in an assured mastery over the
lower nature, what Paul called the σάρξ. The
external forces under whose dominion men had
groaned included Sin; and these all had been
paralysed or were being paralysed (καταργούμενοι)
by Christ. It was therefore with a consciousness
of possessing and confronting a beaten foe that
they challenged the powers of evil. The ethical
ideal which apart from religion may appear quite
hopeless of realisation is nevertheless not wholly
beyond the reach of those who live ἐν καινότητι
ζωῆς under new conditions of Life and are im-
pelled by the Spirit. But if not so, then not so.
That is the first limitation.

The second has to do of course with the area of
human life and conduct to which the teaching of
the New Testament applies. Apart from the great
principles the application of which to questions of
conduct to-day we are left to discover for ourselves, the direct teaching is limited to situations
which were familiar in the first century. Many of
these of course are part of the perennial experience
of every individual and of society at all times. But
the opportunities of human life have since then been
indefinitely increased and with them the responsi-
bilities. And concerning many of these we look for
direct guidance from the New Testament, in vain.

We may take first the antithesis between what the Germans call *Weltverneinung* and *Weltbejahung*, world-renunciation and world-assertion, which troubles some people from time to time. Concerning this there is very little evidence. What there is seems to point to the antithesis being an artificial one. If I have interpreted the teaching of Jesus correctly, He recognised that some of His followers might be required by their calling, their function in the Kingdom, to deny themselves much that was permitted to others. For these others their calling by God did not involve these limitations. He pronounced the one who was least in the Kingdom of Heaven greater than the most typically ascetic figure of the time. St Paul is more explicit, and points in the same direction. In 1 Cor. v. 10 he uses as a *reductio ad absurdum* the suggestion "in that case you must needs quit the world". And the fourth Gospel appears to say the last word on the subject when it reports our Lord as saying, "Ye are in the world, but not of the world".[1]

On the question of the relation of the Christian to the civil power there is in the New Testament more material, but it is difficult to interpret and still more difficult to apply to the conditions of our own time. When our Lord said, "Render unto

[1] So Frick, *l.c.* p. 13: "Jesus sees in God the Creator, and for him there exists, without any half-heartedness or tension, a union of thankful enjoyment of human joys with a high earnestness of moral life".

Caesar the things that are Caesar's; and unto God the things that are God's", he certainly recognised the existence of the two spheres, the civil and the religious, and the obligations which were to be met in each of them. But His words throw no light on their relative importance or on the duty of His followers in the event of contradictory claims being made by the State and by conscience. The words must be taken in close connection with the question to which they are an answer, "Is it lawful to give tribute unto Caesar, or not?" And there is a touch of impatience in the answer, impatience with the political casuistry of the questioners. Of course pay tribute to Caesar. The money is his, and you pay it for value received. You are straining at a gnat when you raise the question. For the acknowledgment of Caesar's rule involved in paying the tribute is a trumpery thing compared with other forms of acknowledgment which you make every day. Besides you must pay to Caesar. What really matters is to see to it that you render to God what belongs to Him; for that lies entirely within your choice.

St Paul deals fully and explicitly with the subject in Ro. xiii. "The powers that be are ordained of God." It is tempting to suppose, as some have done, that His teaching here may be limited to the civil powers which were actually in control at the time He wrote, the Roman Empire in the fifties and its administrators. But the opinion that he is laying down general propositions applicable to other times and to other forms of government is not only in closer accordance with his language, but is supported by the fact that the same position had been taken up by earlier writers. Thus in Wisdom (vi. 1) we find, "Give ear, ye kings, and understand; your power was given unto you by the Lord, and your dominion by the Most High"; and in Enoch xlvi. 5, "He will put down the kings from their thrones...because they do not thankfully acknowledge whence the kingdom was bestowed upon them". The difference of course is that Paul draws from the same principle the inference that Christians owe implicit obedience to the civil power.

If that be so, then his teaching must be modified in the light of later experience and altered circumstances. One may well doubt whether he himself would have written in the same strain ten years later, when the Empire turned persecutor and especially when the worship of the Emperor came to be rigidly enforced. At the time when he was writing, the civil power of Rome, whether imperial or provincial, presented itself to him only as a beneficent influence. In particular, it had on several occasions protected him and his fellow-Christians against being rabbled by the Jews. Rome was still acting as the "restrainer" (2 Thess.

ii. 7), and Paul had good reason for saying, "He is
the minister of God to thee for good". At the same
time, in the reasons which he gives for obedience
to the civil power he opens the door to a revision
of his opinion, should the rulers become a terror
to the good work and cease to be a terror to the
evil.

On the whole, Paul left this question where it
could not stay, the question of woman's status in
the family only partially solved, and the question
of slavery untouched.

The same must be said of the whole field of industrial and economic problems, although here,
much more obviously than in the case of the other
problems I have mentioned, a very great deal
could be accomplished by a wide and continuous
application of Christ's simple command, "Thou
shalt care for thy neighbour as for thyself". It
requires only a slight acquaintance with some of
our heavy industries or with some forms of domestic
service to realise how promptly some of the worst
conditions would be changed by this. But even a
similarly slight acquaintance with the human type,
which has in many cases both the power and the
opportunity, points to the conclusion that nothing
short of "a change of heart" will bring about the
result. When one studies the most up-to-date books
on industrial management, and the conditions of
labour, the dreams of our economic idealists, the

thought which comes to one's mind is often that expressed in Mrs Browning's words, "Speak thou, availing Christ, and fill this pause"

That brings me lastly to the most difficult and heart-searching question as to the duty of Christians when their country is at war. For them to fight, is it right or is it wrong? I feel bound to give my opinion that we shall search the New Testament in vain for any direct injunction bearing on the subject. The evidence which is appealed to is very scanty and it is ambiguous, in the sense that when it is all gathered together and looked at impartially it lends such support as it gives at all about equally to both opinions. So both sides appeal to it.

To many of course it appears that the question is settled by our Lord's command that we should love our enemies. And we do seem to be flying in the face of that commandment when either we ourselves or we through others take every means to kill them. Shylock asks, "Hates any man the thing he would not kill?" We have to turn the question round and ask, "Kills any man the thing he does not hate?" And I am afraid the answer since our late experience must be "Yes". I say, I am afraid, not because for one moment I think that hatred is an excuse for killing, but because this was a horror of war which was newly brought home to us fifteen years ago, that it is or has become not a hot-blooded but a cold-blooded thing. Of course in the moment of battle, especially in hand to hand fighting, there must be hot blood, and possibly what may be described as hate. But part of the tragedy of the late war was that for months and years hundreds of thousands of men did all they could to destroy one another whose only motive was that they considered it to be their duty. Witness the fraternising which took place between the private soldiers on both sides when the first Christmas came round, which so annoyed and alarmed their officers. Witness the desperate and continuous efforts made on both sides to stimulate hatred of the enemy, even by invented stories of his cruelty. Witness the phrase one heard so often used by our soldiers of their 'enemy', "He's only doing his job, same as we". The question before us is not a simple question of antithesis between love and hate.

But Jesus said, "Love your enemies". And many of us would gladly find there a sure and simple answer to the question. But if we would be honest with ourselves and towards Him, we must admit that these words do not cover the case in point. Men do not become 'enemies' in the sense in which Jesus uses the word by the mere fact that their respective governments declare war on one another. It is true that this is the only sense in which most of us are conscious of having "enemies".

But personal enmity which is what indeed He refers to was in His day all too common a thing. Envy, malice, treachery had opportunities of injuring the individual which are much reduced to-day. And that it is to enemies in that sense that our Lord refers is surely plain from the context, whether we take the report of Matthew or that of Luke. "Love your enemies, and pray for them that persecute you": "Love your enemies, do good to them that hate you, bless them that curse you, and pray for them that insult you" (Lk. vi. 27). That is not the way in which anyone would describe those whom war has made our enemies.

The situation is the same when we look for guidance to Paul. "If thine enemy hunger, feed him; if he thirst, give him drink." Obviously, the enemy here is in great straits. He is not an assailant. He is not armed. He is helpless. What Paul says applies with full force to prisoners of war; but it throws no light on what is to be done in face of an armed foe.

These are serious limitations. They would be more serious still if the New Testament were to be looked on as offering a complete code of ethics. The conclusion is that in the first place the New Testament does not offer such a code, in the second place God has thrown upon us the responsibility of discovering the answer to these and other problems. Some of them have been settled.

The question of slavery has been settled in theory, and, to a very large extent, in practice. Of the other questions some are nearer to solution than others. The responsibility has been thrown upon the individual, but upon the individual as a member of the community, and especially upon the community. It is part of the task of the Christian Church, the Ecclesia.

This appears to be in the first place the meaning of our Lord's words addressed to the disciples in Mt. xviii. 18. Here I know that I tread upon debatable ground, ground which I have no intention of debating. But whatever interpretation we may adopt of the earlier passage (xvi. 19) in which similar powers are assigned to St Peter, the words in xviii. 18 are certainly addressed to a group; I know what Dr Gore has said about those who take for granted that the commission was given to the Church as a whole as indicating "a considerable amount of wilfulness of mind". But I ask myself, to whom then was it given? Not on this occasion, or according to this report, to Peter, but to a group. What group then? Dr Gore (and many others) would have us understand the Apostles. But St Matthew as we all know has very little to say about Apostles. His solitary reference to them is eight chapters back in x. 2. It would be easier to suggest the Twelve or "the twelve disciples"; but again they have only been mentioned twice, and the last case was in xi. 1. If we take this context as beginning at xvi. 1, we find that the recurring description of the followers of Jesus is "the disciples", which occurs some eleven times in all. Of course "the disciples" no doubt includes the Twelve, but it would be difficult to maintain that it includes no one else. And it is surely significant that the verse which immediately precedes this one contains the word Ecclesia, "Tell it to the Church".

Unless we are prepared to admit with many critical scholars that the use of the word here and in chapter xviii is due to the Evangelist and not to our Lord, we must take it to be a deliberate adoption of the word so familiar to readers of the LXX, and a clear indication of our Lord's intention to 're-found' (as Dr Gore puts it) the old Church of Israel, or as I should say, to bring into existence a new People of God, a new Church. And as far as I can see, it is to this new Ecclesia, the assembled People of God, whether it be the whole body, or whether it be two or three met together in Christ's name, that power and authority are given to decide what is permitted and what is forbidden. Of course the radius of their authority will depend partly on their number, partly on their representative character, or (to use a phrase of Dr Rawlinson's) on their having "an adequately Christian mind". It is to the Ecclesia in some sense that the task is assigned and the power given.

How then are we to set about it? I do not think that we shall look very hopefully to the ecclesiastics. They are too busy with other things. But we should be able to look to the Ecclesiola within the Ecclesia, the group of Christian men and women who are united by a common loyalty to Christ and a common desire to ascertain what is the will of God in these matters. They would gather not for heated debate, to issue in hasty resolutions, nor yet as coteries of those who wearing the same political or ecclesiastical label indicate that their minds are already made up. The first essentials are humility and the absence of party-spirit. The next is patience. Each time they met they would take measures to fulfil the conditions of being "taught in Christ". Some will say that it is a Quaker Meeting that I am describing. Be it so. For I remind you that there is no body of Christians which has been so successful in discovering new ethical applications of Christianity as the Society of Friends, especially in connection with industrial relations. Though even they have not settled the question of a Christian's duty in war. And we do not need to be Quakers in order to follow their method of ascertaining the will of God. All I wish is to remind you of what was St Paul's belief and seems to have been his experience, that this was the method of ethical discovery, the method of reaching a common mind, which was in fact the mind of Christ, that it was possible to ascertain the Will of God.

And meanwhile, are there not certain matters of importance regarding which the Church has been led into truth, conclusions which cannot like the conclusion about slavery be put into the form of legislation, but which nevertheless it might be possible, and it might be well, to make known as an indubitable part of the Christian ethic? They would be none the worse for being thrown into the form of commandments, though there would be no external authority behind them. The world wants to know what we stand for, and we do stand for some things which are either not expressed at all or not clearly expressed in Scripture. Suppose we try to put some of these things down, as accepted in principle, though open to amendment in form.

Thou shalt not in any wise exploit thy man-servant or thy maid-servant, his time, his talents or his health, but in every thing encourage him to make full use of his opportunities of self-development and self-realisation.

This would need a corollary. *Thou shalt not in any thing cheat thine employer of the service thou hast promised him, or of the energy and intelligence that are needed for the performance of thy work.*

Thou shalt not indulge any appetite, however natural,

*at the cost of injury to the health or character or the
dignity of a fellow-creature for whom Christ died.*

Should anyone be inclined to say that these are
mere commonplaces, I reply that only shows that
they do really register the common Christian
mind; but on the other hand, they do not represent
either the theory or the practice of the world
that knows not Christ. By whom might such commandments be promulgated? If the Pope were
moved to use his high position for this end, it
would be putting his infallibility to a worthy use.
Failing him it might be the Primate of England,
after full consultation and agreement with the representatives of the other Christian communions in
the country. I conceive of its being done at the
close of a great service in St Paul's Cathedral,
when the Archbishop would promulgate certain
much needed inferences from the twin commandment of Christ, saying, "Thus it seemed good to
the Holy Spirit and to us".

Detached Notes

p. 7. "Authority represents that part of religion which we have not assimilated." INGE.

"The instruction may and does come from without, both in morals and religion, but the authority which seals it is within, the inward spiritual consciousness which constitutes the life both in religion and morality." THOMAS ERSKINE.

p. 10. "The full significance of what should be meant by God as a person depends on our success in passing beyond mere imperatives for life and a mere Legal Potentate for its environment." JOHN OMAN.

p. 23. "It is not so much our neighbour's interest as our own that we should love him." BP WILSON.

p. 37. "If sin is ignored, Christianity becomes unintelligible." INGE.

p. 62. "The radical character of these sayings is completely explained by the desire to destroy the uttermost roots of vindictiveness and lust for revenge." WINDISCH.

p. 62. "The more you beat Fritz by becoming like him, the more he has won." QUILLER-COUCH.

p. 78. The Law means "for the Jew almost what Christ means for the Christian." MONTEFIORE.

p. 84. "A formal juridical release would not have satisfied Paul, and thenceforward became irrelevant." WICHMANN.

p. 95. Ambition to please God. Cf. 1 Jo. iii. 22; 1 Clem. ii. 2, "an insatiable desire for noble living"; xli. 12, "let each one be pleasing to God".

p. 111. "Truth is that which by causing us to act this way or that way makes us accomplish our purpose." UNAMUNO.

p. 113. "Religion of the spirit is the only possible hygiene of the soul, because it counsels men to withdraw the sting of *possessiveness* out of their passions, and thus by removing anxiety to render them serene." WALTER LIPPMANN.

p. 117. "Condemnation of fornication was a novelty in the Christian religion." BERTRAND RUSSELL.

p. 124. "Virginity may seem a virile energy in its angelic liberty, pre-requisite to the perfection of some high personality." ROBERT BRIDGES.

p. 132. Limitations. See Barry, *Relevance of Christianity*, pp. 51, 76.

p. 140. "England's inability to hate is her trump card in the game of life." IAN HAMILTON.

Index of Quotations